Modern-(

Kotaka
Minamoto-no
Sadayasu Sadao

An Appreciation and History
of his *Kenjutsu* Style

櫻井派甲源（甲斐源氏）一刀流剣道

Christopher M. Clarke
with contributions from
Dr. Thomas Sovik

This book is dedicated to

Kotaka Sukesaburo Minamoto-no Sadayasu Sadao

To his family:
Hisako, Takuma, Tomoko, Yuji, and the late Noriko.

And to his students, especially the late

Craig Campbell
Donald Yehling and
William Dvorine

Front cover photo courtesy of Ms Hisako Kotaka.

Title page: Calligraphy—"*Sakurai-ha Kogen (kai Genji) Itto-ryu kendo.*"

Preface
Hisako Kotaka

I am very grateful to Dr. Christopher M. Clarke, Dr. Tom Sovik, and Sadao's other *kenjutsu* students for preparing this book to remember his life and *kendo* teaching, and to commemorate his passing.

From early in his life, the study of Japanese swordsmanship was one of Sadao's passions. He took very seriously his legacy as a descendant of a *samurai* family and his responsibility to remember and pass along *Kogen Itto-ryu*. He was delighted to have a group of people around him who shared his passion and were eager to learn from him. His children and I are glad to see that he had such a positive impact on his students and that they remember him so fondly. We hope that through his students his enthusiasm for the martial arts will continue here in his adopted country.

Sincerely,

Hisako Kotaka

Preface
David Diguangco

Kotaka Sukesaburo (Minamotono) Sadayasu Sadao, *shodai soke* of the *Sakurai-ha Kogen Itto-ryu* and headmaster of the United States Classical Kendo Federation, passed from this world on the 5th of August 2013. Many have been touched by the life and teaching of this gentleman; a privileged few have had the opportunity to study deeply and to be forever changed.

We are most gratefully indebted to Christopher M. Clarke, retired President and Chief Instructor of the Shorin-ryu Karatedo and Kobudo Association of America, for assembling this volume in memory of Dr. Kotaka. Through this work, all of us—who hold individual bits and pieces of the history and memories of our teacher—will gain a truer and clearer understanding of the *soke*.

Let us continue forward with our training, and let us never fail to live up to the expectations of our teacher.

David Diguangco
Soke, Sakurai-ha Kogen Itto-ryu
Ogden, Utah
16 June 2014

4

Table of Contents

Introduction

Overleaf: The author (right) with fellow *kenshi*, Joe Doles (now a veterinarian in the Cleveland area) training in Kotaka Sadao *Sensei*'s *dojo* around 1975.

As a former student of Kotaka Sadao, Ph.D., *Okuden, Kogen Itto-ryu Kenjutsu*, I was deeply saddened to hear of his death at the age of 80 on August 5, 2013. I had not seen Kotaka *Sensei* in many years, but had followed his efforts to establish a strong following of students and teachers dedicated to the pre-World War II techniques and ethos of traditional Japanese martial arts. I had observed the often unfair criticism he suffered as a result, as well as the amazed accounts of those who actually had the privilege of crossing swords with him. I was also familiar with the tragedies in his personal life and his sad decline in his later years.

Kotaka *Sensei* was one of the last true *samurai* spirits and he will be sorely missed. As a tribute to him, and to help try to set the record straight, I have put together this book. Not everyone will agree with everything I write, nor would Kotaka *Sensei*. He was, for example, a stout defender of the *Shinsen-gumi*, the "police force" and organization created by defenders of the Shogunate against the forces of imperial restoration and the introduction of Western ideas. I'm afraid history has drawn a rather bleaker and more negative verdict on these individuals, their methods, and their impact on society. No one, however, could disagree with his appreciation of their skill as swords-men, their personal courage, or their no-nonsense approach to fighting.

Throughout his *kendo* career, Kotaka *Sensei* maintained that no-nonsense approach. He had little use—other than as entertainment—for the "*chanbara*" style of sword fighting that attracted so many Westerners who watched Japanese movies, made up "Japanese sword-fighting" routines for martial arts competitions, or loved the "*manga*" version of the old *samurai*. His swordsmanship was plain but deep, spiritual but not showy, brutally effective without being brutal. These values were an extension of the swordsmanship that emerged from the last battles of the *samurai*, including the styles of the *Shinsengumi* from which he claimed stylistic descent.

Questions have also been raised about Kotaka *Sensei*'s *bona fides* and the connection of his style to Japan. The stylistic issues are probably unanswerable: although he undoubtedly learned his pre-war *kenjutsu* from a teacher influenced by the *Kogen Itto-ryu* style, a small remnant of which remains active in Japan, the techniques he taught bore little resemblance to those taught by that style today, and the seniors of the style in Japan professed to know nothing of Kotaka *Sensei,* his style, or his *kendo* lineage. Nonetheless, no one who ever had the opportunity to face *Sensei* on the *dojo* floor ever left with any questions about his ability or anything but the highest admiration for his skill. *Sensei* might not be pleased with my conclusions after investigating his connection to Japan's *Kogen Itto-ryu,* but I have done my best to go where the evidence led me.

Finally, *Sensei* had many serious students over the years. Unfortunately, I never had the opportunity to meet or train with most of them. I was one of the first to study with *Sensei*—from about 1973-78—before he began to teach at Ohio State University. But I had left Columbus for a new job in Washington, D.C. before most of them came along. I left well before he set up the "Classical Kendo Federation." No doubt, each of his students would have different interpretations of some of the points I discuss in this book. I know that after I left, *Sensei* introduced a number of techniques he had reconstructed from his pre-War training—our early practice consisted almost entirely of the standard Japanese sets of *iaido* and *kendo* "sparring," as well as the common two-person *Nihon Kendo-no-kata*—so not even our training experiences would have been the same.

In preparing this book, I have attempted to contact a number of his senior students from later years. Sadly, in at least three cases, I reached out just too late. In the summer of 2013, I attempted to reach Dr. William Dvorine, *yodan* in *kendo, iaido,* and *jodo,* but called just weeks after he had passed away. In the spring of 2014, I tried to contact my old friend, Craig Campbell, of Columbus, Ohio, one of Kotaka *Sensei's* most senior students and closest collaborators, only to find that he had died a week earlier. Likewise, Donald Yehling died even while I was reaching out to get his input for this book. I would like to extend my condolences to their families and express my regret for missing the opportunity to discuss *Sensei* with them. For those of us still here who were honored to have trained with Kotaka *Sensei*, his spirit will live on.

I would also be sadly remiss if I did not acknowledge the help and encouragement of Dr. Thomas Sovik, who not only provided an outstanding set of recollections of his many years with Kotaka *Sensei* for inclusion in the book, but spent an enormous amount of time—while facing a number of personal troubles and losses—to communicate repeatedly with me about the book, to contact others and attempt to gain their participation and approval, and most of all to provide the moral support that this was a project well worth doing. ありがとうございます (*Arigato gozaimasu!*)

I would like to express my deep appreciation to Mrs. Hisako Kotaka, *sensei*'s widow, both for her kindness when I trained at their house some 40 years ago and for her assistance in preparing this book. Despite facing a number of travails in addition to the loss of her husband of some 50 years, she graciously responded to a number of letters, emails, and telephone calls and provided me with a treasure trove of materials about and by Kotaka Sadao. すみません, 恐れ入ります (*Sumimasen, Osoreirimasu*).

Christopher M. Clarke
Huntingtown, MD
July 2014

Kotaka Sukesaburo Minamoto-no Sadayasu Sadao

(1933-2013)

Overleaf: Kotaka Sadao *Sensei* in *kendo bogu* probably in the 1990s.

Background

D r. Kotaka Sadao, was born on January 5, 1933 in Hankou, central China, to a family of distinguished *samurai* lineage on both the paternal and maternal sides.[1] He traced his ancestry back to the "Seiwa Genji," the most successful and powerful line of the Japanese Minamoto clan that were descended from Emperor Seiwa (850-878), the 56th emperor of Japan. (See pages 26-35) Many of the most famous Minamoto warriors belong to this line, including Minamoto Yoshiie, also known as *"Hachiman-taro,"* or the "God of War"; Minamoto no Yoritomo, the founder of the Kamakura shogunate; and Ashikaga Takauji, the founder of the Ashikaga shogunate. Tokugawa Ieyasu (1543-1616), founder of the Tokugawa shogunate, also claimed descent from this lineage.

Kotaka was born in China because his father was stationed there as a member of the Japanese foreign service. In about 1935, the family moved back to Tokyo when his father was reassigned to the foreign ministry, and the three-year old Sadao was enrolled in a local *kendo* school. The next year, his father was assigned to the embassy in Beijing (then called Peking) and Sadao began to train more seriously in *kendo* and *iaido* under the embassy's resident martial arts instructor, Konagaya *Sensei,* the commissioner of the Japanese police force in Beijing. Konagaya, who ran the *Butoku-Kan Dojo,* in the embassy complex, was a master (*kaiden* 8th *dan*) in the *"Kogen Itto-ryu"* school of *kendo,* and also an instructor of *judo, kyodo* (archery), *jodo* (short staff), *sojutsu* (spear), and *Hojojutsu* (the art of tying up a prisoner).[2]

Sadao's father was transferred back to Tokyo apparently in 1942, when Sadao was in fourth grade, or about the age of 9 or 10. Sometime later, his family was evacuated from the capital—which was being bombed by American Army Air Forces—to Yamanashi Prefecture, the ancestral lands of the Kai Genji clan and the former stronghold of Takeda Shingen, about 65 miles west of Tokyo.

Yamanashi is a land-locked, mountainous area that

includes the northern half of the iconic Mount Fuji and the Fuji Five Lakes region. It was while attending middle school in Yamanashi prefecture that Kotaka met his principle *kendo* master, Sakurai Gen'noshin Fumitaka (c.1853-1954), a 9th *dan kaiden*.

桜井 え之進

(Sakurai Gen'noshin in Kotaka Sadao's handwriting.)

According to Dr. Kotaka, Sakurai was one of the youngest and last members of the famous (or notorious) Shinsengumi, the forces who resisted the attempt to overthrow the 250 year old shogunate and restore power to Emperor Meiji.[3] (See Part III below.) The Shinsengumi, which lasted from 1863 -1869, were among the most feared swordsmen of the day; they trained intensively and for the real combat they regularly faced against bandits, underworld figures, *ronin* (masterless *samurai*) and imperial supporters.[4] Sakurai was also the chief instructor in middle school of Japanese literature, Chinese literature and calligraphy, history and ethics.

Dr. Kotaka trained under Sakurai Gen'nosuke Fumitaka as a youth, when Sakurai would have already been at least well into his 80s. Teaching of the traditional Japanese martial arts—especially swordsmanship, which was associated in the minds of the American occupation with the pre-War militarism of Japan—was banned. Nonetheless, Sakurai *Sensei* continued "to teach and practice underground," according to Kotaka. In 1995, he recalled that "We would pretend to be doing foil fencing whenever the Americans would come by, and then back to *Kendo* when they left."[5] According to Kotaka:

> Sakurai *Sensei* required everyone to learn *kendo, iai-do, kata, tai-yoho* (similar to *Aikido*, for unarmed combat). Like most traditional martial arts instructors, he taught using the visual method, he would show how a technique was done, and he expected you to do it. Not much verbal instruction.[6]

He claimed to have trained with Sakurai until he was a junior in college (thus likely around 20-21 years of age), when

16

Sakurai would have been in his mid-90s.* This, and Kotaka's claim to teach and to be the inheritor of Sakurai's "*Kogen Itto-ryu*," later led to questions and controversy.

Professional life

Kotaka apparently attended the prestigious Tokyo University.[8] He moved to the U.S. in January 1959, to pursue graduate research at the University of California, Berkeley.[9] He seems to have been pursuing his graduate degree under the auspices of the Institute of Plant Biochemistry of the Tokyo University of Education while attached to UCAL Berkeley's Air Ion Laboratory, Department of Bacteriology, during the early 1960s. He received his Ph.D. in biochemistry from the Tokyo University of Education sometime after 1965.[10] (See Appendix A for a list of his professional papers.)

During this period (roughly 1959-1965), according to his own account, he "did not have time to practice *kendo*," but practiced *judo* at the university gym with "a friend who was champion of [the] All-Japan College Judo Tournament, 1957 and 1958."[11] *Sensei* became an accomplished *judoka*, ranked *sandan* or *yodan*, though he had long since ceased to practice when I trained with him.[12]

He spent a year in 1964-1965 in Japan working on a joint research project with the University of Ibaraki. He returned to the U.S. a year later, where he took up the practice of modern *shinai kendo* at a *dojo* near Berkeley, California,[13] training under Miyata Yoshinori *Sensei* (6th *dan*), one of the founders of the *dojo* in the early 1950s and a pioneer of post-War *kendo* in the U.S.♦

---

* Sakurai apparently died in 1954 at roughly the age of 100, according to hand-written notes by Kotaka in the author's possession and remarks to the author by Kotaka *Sensei*. In a 1995 interview, Kotaka said Sakurai died "in the late 1950s."[7]

♦ Kotaka *Sensei* wrote out Miyata *Sensei*'s name and rank in Japanese, but confusingly wrote down next to his name both the characters for *kyoshi* and *hanshi*. It is not clear which title he held at the time, but *hanshi* was usually reserved for grades higher than 6th *dan*. Paper in the author's collection.

17

Map of Japan

Regions and Prefectures of Japan

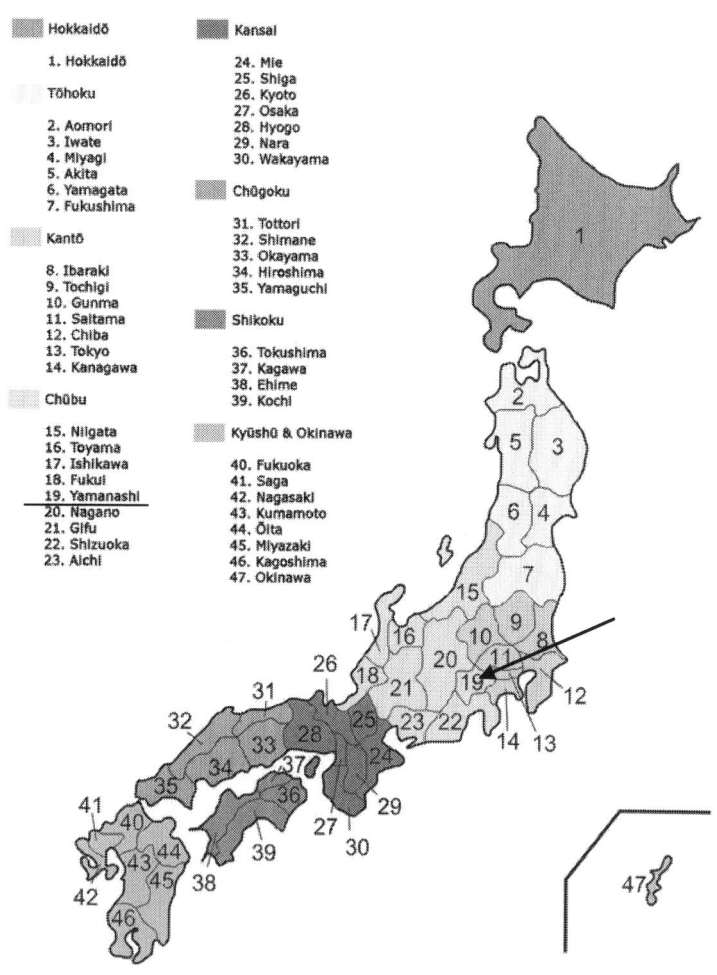

Hokkaidō
1. Hokkaidō

Tōhoku
2. Aomori
3. Iwate
4. Miyagi
5. Akita
6. Yamagata
7. Fukushima

Kantō
8. Ibaraki
9. Tochigi
10. Gunma
11. Saitama
12. Chiba
13. Tokyo
14. Kanagawa

Chūbu
15. Niigata
16. Toyama
17. Ishikawa
18. Fukui
19. Yamanashi
20. Nagano
21. Gifu
22. Shizuoka
23. Aichi

Kansai
24. Mie
25. Shiga
26. Kyoto
27. Osaka
28. Hyogo
29. Nara
30. Wakayama

Chūgoku
31. Tottori
32. Shimane
33. Okayama
34. Hiroshima
35. Yamaguchi

Shikoku
36. Tokushima
37. Kagawa
38. Ehime
39. Kochi

Kyūshū & Okinawa
40. Fukuoka
41. Saga
42. Nagasaki
43. Kumamoto
44. Ōita
45. Miyazaki
46. Kagoshima
47. Okinawa

Source: http://commons.wikimedia.org/wiki/Atlas_of_Japan.

18

Yamanashi Prefecture

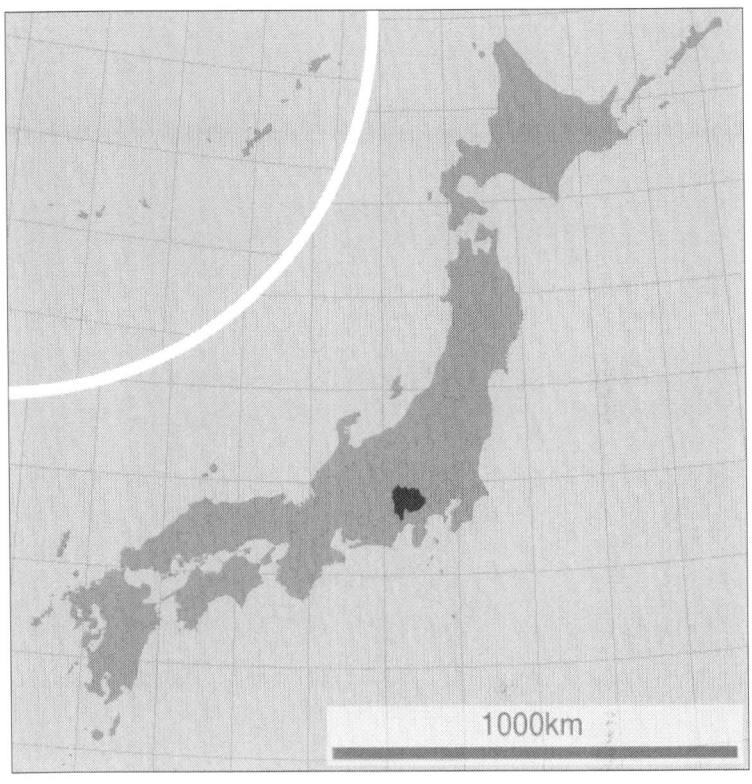

Source: http://en.wikipedia.org/wiki/File:Map_of_Japan_with_highlight_
on_19_Yamanashi_prefecture.svg.

Dr. Kotaka moved to Columbus, Ohio in the early 1970s and began working at Chemical Abstracts, a service associated with the American Chemical Society and affiliated with the Biochemistry Department of The Ohio State University. He also worked at the Batelle Memorial Institute, a private nonprofit applied science and technology development company headquartered in Columbus, Ohio. He was widely respected as a scientist and was listed in the prestigious *American Men & Women of Science: A Biographical Directory of Today's leaders in Physical, Biological, and Related Sciences* (12th edition, 1971-1973). Dr. Kotaka was also a poet (in Japanese), regularly contributing verses to several publications.

Kendo practice and teaching

In the early 1970s, Kotaka *Sensei* taught a few students (including the author) privately in his two-car-plus garage, which he had converted to a *dojo*. Around 1979 or 1980, he opened a *Kendo-Iaido* Club at the Physical Education building at The Ohio State University,[14] where he taught a number of students who later became well-known swordsmen and who opened *Kogen Itto-ryu* schools around the country. (See pages 39-42 for a partial list of Kotaka *Sensei*'s students.)

Kotaka Sadao was ranked *godan* (5th *dan*), *renshi* by the All-U.S. Kendo Federation in 1974 and 6th *dan* in 1981. (See following page.) He was a founding member and at one time vice president and/or secretary-general of the Midwest Kendo Association, where he had an excellent reputation.[15]

In the 1980s, Kotaka began to distance himself from the mainstream *kendo* movement, complaining that it had become bound up with too many constricting rules, lost the spirit of pre-War *kendo,* and become more like "figure skating," (his words) with the search for "style" and "easy points" (my words) such as *kote*, which counted for only a half-point in his system.[16]

In the mid-1990s, Kotaka established the tax-exempt, not-for-profit United States Classical Kendo Federation to teach

Kotaka Sadao's *Kendo* Diplomas

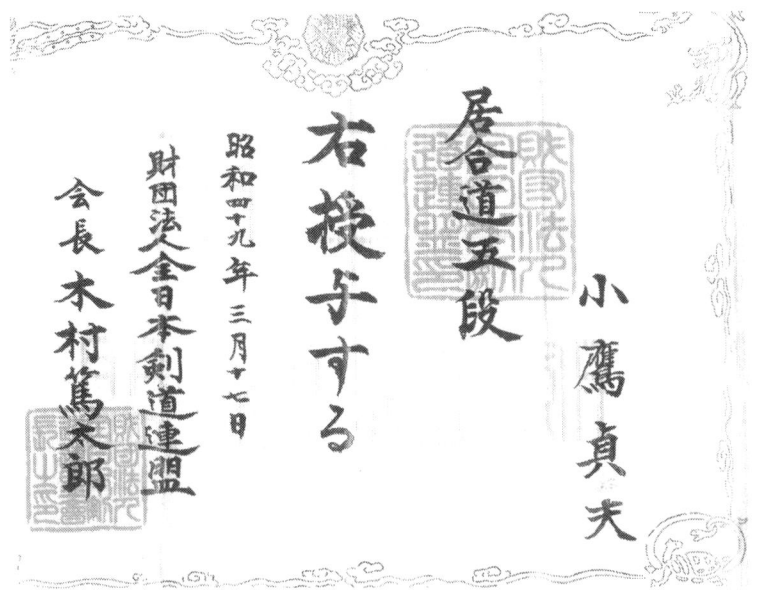

Kotaka Sadao, Above: *Iaido Godan*, "*Showa* 49" (1974);
Below, *Kendo Rokudan* (1981).

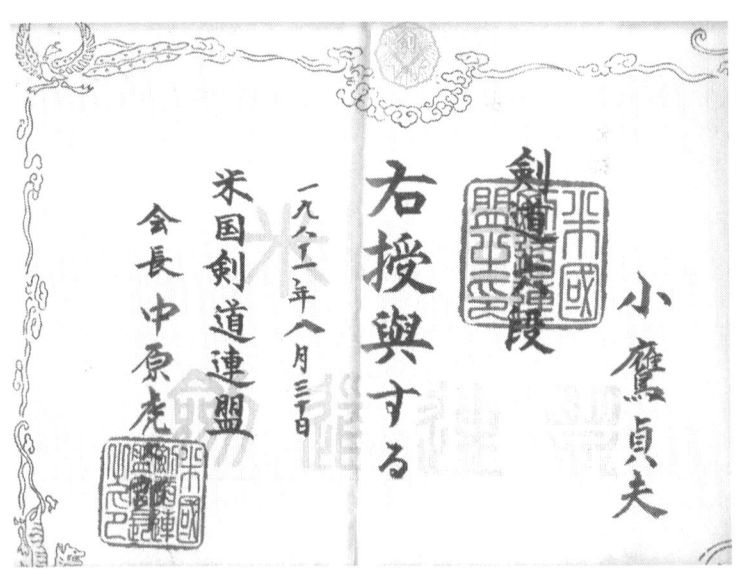

Diplomas courtesy of Hisako Kotaka.

21

and propagate what he saw as traditional *kenjutsu* and *budo*.[17] This included not only *iaido, shinai kendo,* and the standard Japanese *kendo* federation two-man *Nihon Kendo-no-kata,* but a series of old-style two-person drills using special *"onigote"* ("Devil's gloves," heavily padded hand and wrist protectors) and a unique *bokken,* straighter and heavier than the standard wooden sword. To his most senior students, he also passed along some of the self-defense techniques he had been taught by Sakurai *Sensei,* and his senior students were even allowed to use such techniques during *kendo* matches. Occasionally, he would engage in matches against more than one opponent. He never attempted to make a living out of teaching *kendo* as far as I know and never asked me to pay tuition.

In the mid-1990s, according to one of his former students, Kotaka suffered from "a health issue that affected his cognitive abilities," for which he underwent surgery.[18] The surgery partially alleviated the symptoms, but Kotaka *Sensei* appears to have developed some form of mental illness in his last years that, as is sadly so often the case, damaged his relationships with family, friends, and students. He also became increasingly concerned about a curse he said had been laid on him and his family. (See below.)

Kotaka *Sensei* retired both from active teaching and practice of *kendo* and from his professional activities around 2006. In 2009, he retired to Clermont, Florida where he died of a heart attack on August 5, 2013.[19]

Family

Kotaka Sadao was married to the former Yuhara Hisako, and the couple had four children: son Takuma P., daughters Noriko J. and Tomoko C., and son Yuji D., all born in California. His kind wife always invited me in for green tea and perhaps a piece of fruit after our workouts in the heat and humidity of summer and the cold of winter in his unheated, un-air-conditioned *dojo*. Tragically, Noriko died of cancer in October 1986 at the young age of 20. She was a beautiful, talented, and promising young lady and her loss was a real tragedy.

I later heard that *Sensei* believed his family was suffering under a curse laid on by someone years ago in Japan.[20] He apparently blamed the curse for the loss of his daughter and hung up his sword for about a year as a sign of mourning.

From time to time, Kotaka *Sensei* suffered health problems, and possibly some residual emotional trauma from the War. At one point, I learned, *Sensei* developed a problem that for a time prevented him from wearing his *bogu*. Eventually, his doctors found he was allergic to the horsehair stuffing of his old *men* or *do* (I'm not sure which). When he traded it for one without horsehair, he was again able to practice. His later years were troubled with emotional and mental health problems which estranged him from many of those who loved and admired him.

Kotaka Sadao (right) engaged in *kendo keiko* with unidentified opponent.

Photo: by Monte Van Paepegham from *Ohio Martial Artist*, August 1985.

23

Kotaka Sadao's Swords

Kotaka *Sensei* was very proud of his swords, especially the one he inherited from his great grandfather's first cousin, Harada Sanosuke, who was one of the leaders of the Shinsengumi. According to sword expert Dr. Philip Fellman, who examined it, it is a

> ... fine Yamashiro blade made by Kaneiwa during the Nambokucho Jidai [Warring States period]. The blade itself, originally an *o-dachi* [long sword], had been shortened to 260 [mm?] in order to be convenient for indoor fighting, and belonged to Kotaka *Sensei*'s great grandfather's first cousin, Harada Sanosuke, who was one of the leaders of the Shinsen Gumi. The blade had a fine *o-kissaki* [large or long tip], beautiful *itame hada* [surface grain pattern] with streaming *ji -nie* [ridge line], *kaen boshi* [a flaming line on the cutting edge of the tip], and despite long usage was still in fine condition. It appears to have a *go-mai tetsu* construction [a thin center of hard steel wrapped in soft steel as its core with a final layer of hard-steel wrapping around for the edge], and while it has a narrow *o-suriage nakago* [a greatly shortened tang], the original *mei* [signature of the sword smith] is still present. The *koshirae* [fittings] are equally striking, being a complete and properly matched set of fine Higo mounts. Both the blade and the mounts reflected a purity of artistic integrity rarely seen today in private collections. Of course, this is Dr. Kotaka's ancestral blade, and one of some historical significance, so perhaps I should not have been so surprised. Still, it is a blade which has a long history, and in the words of Kotaka *sensei*, "It has been through three revolutions" (Nambokucho, Sengoku and Meiji restoration.)

The sword smith, "Kaneiwa was a respected swordsmith in the Mino tradition skilled at creating the eye-catching '*Sanbonsugi hamon*' temper line. This a temper line that 'peaks' on every third wave mimicking the tree line of cedars that grow in the Gifu prefecture."

Altogether, Kotaka Sensei had four fine swords. One was a "*jindachi*" made by Oei Bizen Morimitsu of Osabune. I do not know the

Sources: Interview conducted in 1998 by Dr. Fellman, available on http://listserve.uoguelph.ca/cgi-bin/wa?A2=ind9810&L=iaido-l&D=0&F=P&P=5587, accessed September 16, 2009; "A Kaneiwa Katana" at http://new.uniquejapan.com/a-kaneiwa-katana/.

exact provenance of the sword, but "Oe Bizen" was a school of sword making that went back to at least the mid-1300s. A "*tachi*" or "*dachi*" is generally a longer, larger sword than the *katana* and was fitted to be worn hanging from the belt of an armored warrior, cutting edge down (rather than thrust through the belt, cutting edge up, as with a *katana*.) As a result, the *mei* (signature) was on the opposite side of the tang. Morimitsu of the Oe Bizen school flourished around 1384 as the attached chart shows. Kotaka kept it storied in a *shirosaya*, (or *shirasaya*), a "white" wood mounting consisting of a *saya* and *tsuka* (hilt), employed when a blade was not expected to be used for some time and needs to be stored. These *shirosaya* are externally featureless save for the needed *mekugi-ana* (hole in the hilt) to secure the *nakago* (tang). Such mountings are not intended for actual combat because of the lack of a *tsuba* (guard) and proper handle wrappings.

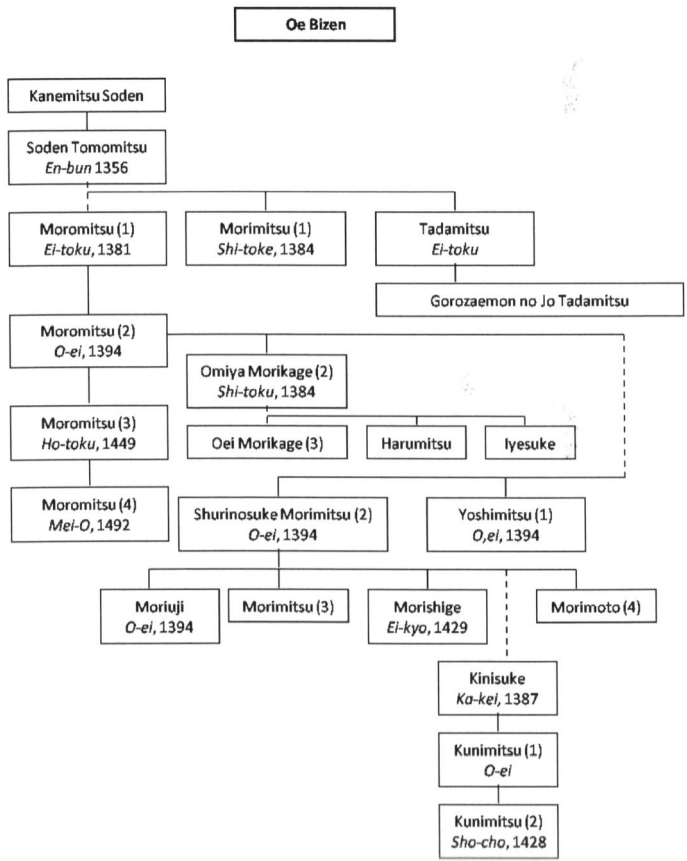

Source: http://www.sho-shin.com/oei.htm. Note: the words in italics under the names represent the Japanese era, or period, names, their way of dating.

25

The Seiwa Genji

The Seiwa Genji were the most successful and powerful line of the Japanese Minamoto clan, a lineage that descended from Emperor Seiwa (912-c.997 AD), the alleged 56th emperor in the line extending back to the legendary Emperor Jimmu (660-585 BC). "Genji" is the more Sinified (Chinese-like) pronunciation of the character that, in Japanese, is usually read as "Minamoto."[21]

The first emperor to grant the surname Minamoto was Emperor Saga (785-842), who reportedly had 49 children, resulting in a significant financial burden on the imperial household. In order to alleviate some of the pressure of supporting his unusually large family, he made many of his sons and daughters nobles instead of royals. He chose the word *minamoto* (meaning "origin") for their new surname in order to signify that the new clan shared the same origins as the royal family.[22] Afterwards, other emperors, including Seiwa, also gave their sons or daughters the name Minamoto.[23] The specific hereditary lines coming from different emperors developed into specific clans referred to by the emperor's name followed by Genji, such as the "Seiwa Genji," "Yamato Genji," and "Settsu Genji." The descendants of the Seiwa Genji founded many of the major noble houses of later times, such as the Tokugawa, Nitta, Hosokawa, and Takeda clans.

Emperor Seiwa (912-c.997)

Like many of Japan's most famous and powerful clans, the Minamoto began as offshoots of non-succeeding sons of an emperor. They moved to the countryside to establish a power base, reclaim and put into use agricultural land, or conquer "barbarians" or Japanese groups that either had rebelled against, or were never under the control of, the imperial house.

Over the generations from the 900s, the Minamoto produced some of Japan's most famous warriors:

- **Minamoto no Yoshiie** (源 義家, 1041-1108) became known as *Hachiman-taro*, or the God of War.[24] The oldest son of Yoriyoshi, Yoshiie was a 7th generation descendant of Seiwa. As commander-in-chief in defense of the north, the first proved himself in the so-called "Early Nine-Years War" (1050-1063, with a three-year truce in the middle) against the Abe clan, and again in the "Later Three-Years War" (1083-1086) against the Kiyohara family. He was considered a paragon of warrior skill and bravery.

Yoshiie, from a triptych by Yoshitoshi Taiso (1839-1892)

Minamoto no Yoritomo

* **Minamoto no Yoritomo** (源 頼朝, 1147-1199) was the
  third son of Yoshitomo, heir as head of the Seiwa Genji.[25]
  Beginning in 1156, factional divisions in the court erupted
  into open warfare within the capital, pitting the current
  emperor and part of the Fujiwara family (who had tradition-
  ally provided wives and regents for the imperial family)
  against the retired emperor and another faction of the Fujiwara. The Seiwa Genji were split between the two factions.
  After two brutal but short wars, the Minamoto were
  defeated, Yoshitomo killed, and Yoritomo exiled. War
  broke out again in 1180, but Yoritomo bided his time,
  building a powerful following in Kamakura, far from the
  imperial capital, Kyoto, which was the focus of the fighting. In the end, through treachery as well as bravery, Yoritomo emerged on top, taking the title *"Shogun,"* establish-
  ing the supremacy of the warrior *samurai* caste, and creating the first *Bakufu* (shogunate, literally "tent government")
  at Kamakura. This began the feudal age in Japan which
  lasted until the mid-19th century.

- **Minamoto no Yoshitsune** ((源 義経, 1159-1189) was perhaps the most famous warrior in Japanese history.[26] He was the ninth son of Yoshitomo and younger brother of Yoritomo. As a baby, he barely escaped being put to death by the victorious Taira clan and was sent to be raised at a monastery in the mountains where he is said to have learned swordsmanship and strategy from the half-human/half-bird *tengu*.[27] In 1180, Yoshitsune heard that Yoritomo had raised an army to fight against the Taira clan which had usurped the power of the emperor. He quickly joined Yoritomo, along with Minamoto no Noriyori, all brothers who had never before met. Together they fought in the last of three conflicts between the rival Minamoto and Taira *samurai* clans, known as the Genpei War. Yoshitsune defeated and killed his rival cousin Minamoto no Yoshinaka at the Battle of Awazu in early 1184, and in the next month defeated the Taira at the Battle of Ichi-no-tani, one of the most famous battles in

Japanese history. In 1185, Yoshitsune defeated the Taira again at the Battle of Yashima in Shikoku and destroyed them at the Battle of Dan-no-ura. Fearing his successful brother, Yoritomo turned against him. Yoshitsune fled, hoping to find refuge in the far north, but eventually was betrayed and run to ground, defeated at the Battle of Koromo River, and forced to commit *seppuku* along with his wife and daughter.

Yoshitsune with his last loyal follower, Benkei,
by Yoshitoshi Taiso.

29

- **Ashikaga Takauji** (足利 尊氏, 1305-1358), the founder of the Ashikaga shogunate, was a descendant of Yoshikane (足利義兼, 1154?-April 5, 1199), who established the Ashikaga branch of the Seiwa Genji.[28] A general of the Kamakura shogunate, he was sent to Kamakura in 1333 to bring an end to the Genko War which had started in 1331. He became increasingly disillusioned with the increasingly effete and ineffective Kamakura rulers, however, Takauji joined the banished Emperor Go-Daigo and his chief defender, Kusunoki Masashige, and seized Kyoto.[28] Soon after, another warlord attacked Kamakura, destroying the shogunate, and Go-Daigo became the *de facto* ruler of Japan, reestablishing the primacy of the Imperial court in Kyoto and starting the so-called Kemmu restoration. The dispossessed *samurai*, however, were not willing to give up power so easily.

Ashikaga Takauji

They rebelled—and Takauji switched sides. After a few setbacks, Takauji defeated Yoshisada again and killed Masashige at the decisive Battle of Minatogawa in 1336, allowing him to seize Kyoto for good. Founding the Ashikaga shogunate in 1338, he ruled until his death in 1358. The famous Zen master Muso Soseki, who enjoyed his favor and worked with him, remarked that Takauji's three important qualities were that he kept his cool in battle and was not afraid of death, he was merciful and tolerant, and he was generous with those below him.[30]

- **Takeda Shingen** (武田 信玄, 1521-1573). Takeda Shingen (his religious name after he took the Buddhist tonsure) was one of the pre-eminent warlords of the late-Warring States (*sengoku*) period of Japan, shortly before the establishment of the Tokugawa shogunate.[31] His adult name was Harunobu. A member of the Kai Genji clan of the Minamoto, he became well known in his youth both for his education—he was a poet of some ability—and his capability on the battlefield. For some reason, however, his father seemed to favor his second son, Nobushige. At the age of 21, Harunobu rebelled against his father, sent him into an unpleasant exile with another clan, and took control of the family and its holdings. This began a 30-year career of warfare and expansion, which initially involved conquering the neighboring province of Shinano. This conquest put him into conflict with Uesugi Kenshin (who was known by a number of other names during his life), a rivalry that

Takeda Shingen

became legendary. The two faced each other on the battlefield five times at the pass of Kawanakajima on their mutual border, battles that have entered Japanese folklore. Famously, during the fourth of the five battles, Uesugi personally broke through Takeda's lines and attacked his rival; Uesugi was armed with a sword, but Takeda defended himself with his *tessen* (iron war fan, a signaling device). Neither appears to have been wounded; Takeda's forces suffered a defeat, but both retreated to their respective strongholds. Later, Takeda Shingen cooperated with another rising warlord—Tokugawa Ieyasu—to conquer the neighboring province of Suruga. Had he lived longer, he might well have proved to be the only *daimyo* who could have successfully opposed the ambitions of Oda Nobunaga (織田 信長, 1534-1582) to unify the country under a single military ruler. Shingen's death has been the subject of a number of tales; the facts are not known for certain. While on campaign in Mikawa Province, he died in camp. Some accounts say he succumbed to an old war wound and some say he died of pneumonia. The most intriguing and romantic version says that while laying siege to the Noda castle at Mikawa, Shingen became enchanted by the sound of a *samurai* on the battlements playing the flute. Coming closer to listen to the music, he was supposedly hit by a sniper, who mortally wounded him.

• **Tokugawa Ieyasu** (徳川家康, 1543-1616), founder of the Tokugawa shogunate, also claimed descent from this lineage. He should need no introduction. He rose from a horrible childhood as a hostage to a rival clan to be a minor warlord, then an ally of the rising Oda Nobunaga, the first of Japan's "three great unifiers," to a key vassal of Toyotomi Hideyoshi. A few years after Hideyoshi's death, he conquered the entire country and placed it under control of his family. The rule of the Tokugawa family would last until the last shogun was deposed in 1868.[32]

The Tokugawa Shogunate

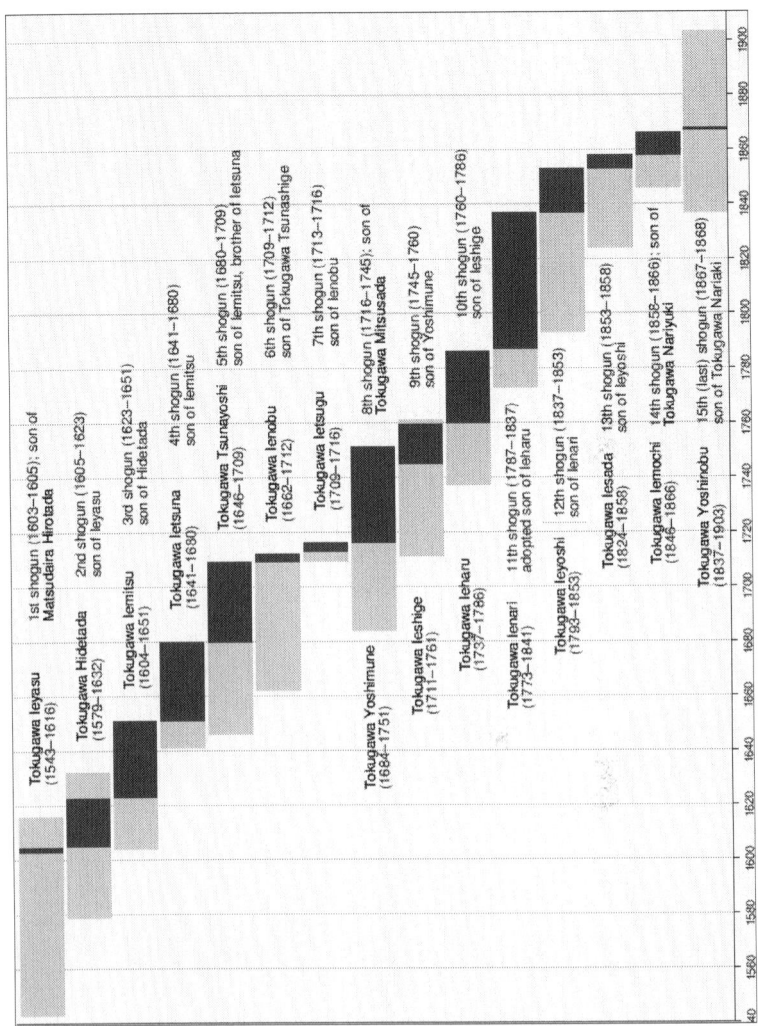

Source: http://en.wikipedia.org/wiki/Tokugawa_shogunate.

33

The Seiwa Genji[32]
清和源氏

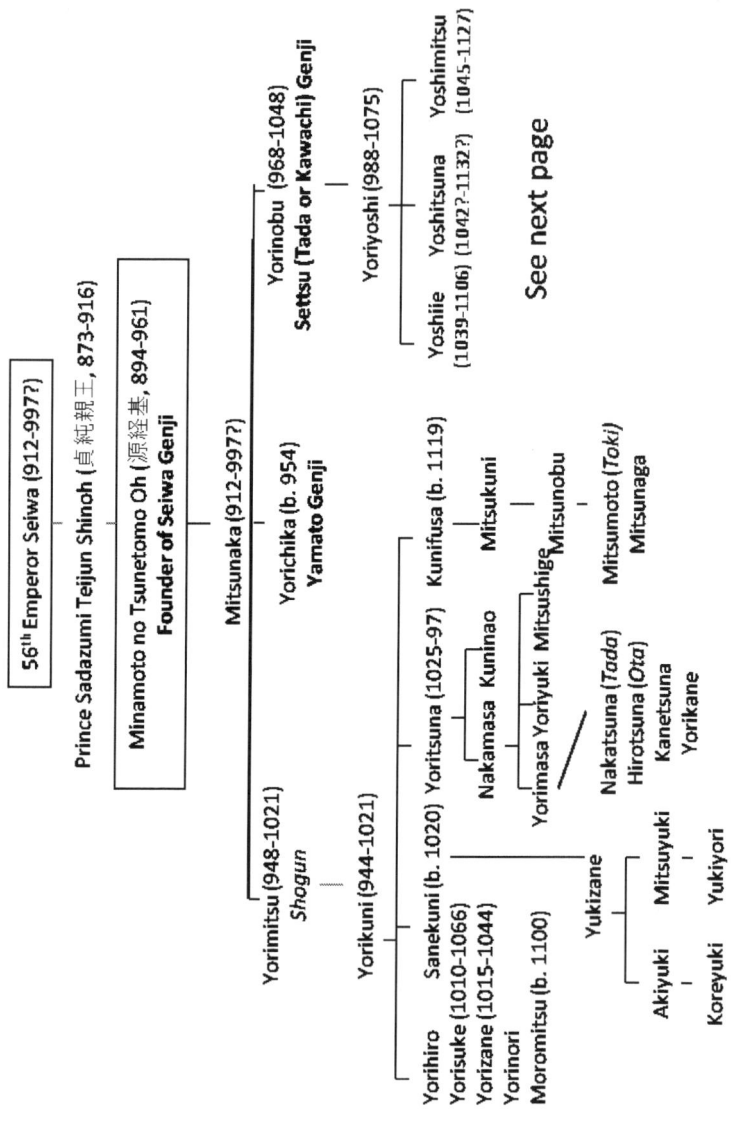

56th Emperor Seiwa (912-997?)

Prince Sadazumi Teijun Shinoh (貞純親王, 873-916)

Minamoto no Tsunetomo Oh (源経基, 894-961)
Founder of Seiwa Genji

Mitsunaka (912-997?)

Yorichika (b. 954)
Yamato Genji

Yorinobu (968-1048)
Settsu (Tada or Kawachi) Genji

Yoriyoshi (988-1075)

Yoshiie (1039-1106)
Yoshitsuna (1042?-1132?)
Yoshimitsu (1045-1127)

See next page

Yorimitsu (948-1021)
Shogun

Yorikuni (944-1021)

Yorihiro
Yorisuke (1010-1066)
Yorizane (1015-1044)
Yorinori
Moromitsu (b. 1100)

Sanekuni (b. 1020)

Yoritsuna (1025-97)

Nakamasa Kuninao

Kunifusa (b. 1119)

Mitsukuni

Yorimasa Yoriyuki Mitsushige Mitsunobu

Nakatsuna (Tada)
Hirotsuna (Ota)
Kanetsuna
Yorikane

Mitsumoto (Toki)
Mitsunaga

Yukizane

Akiyuki Mitsuyuki

Koreyuki Yukiyori

Continued on next page.

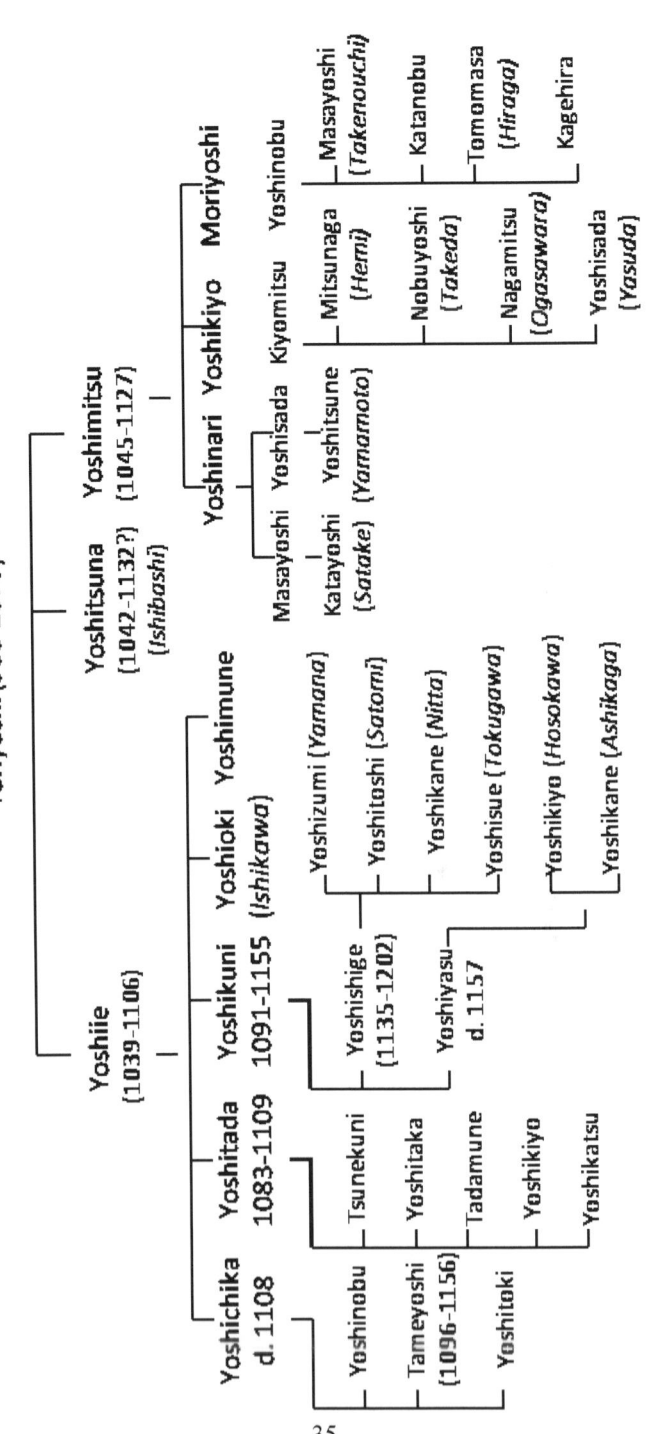

Yoriyoshi (988-1075)

Yoshiie (1039-1106)

Yoshitsuna (1042-1132?) (Ishibashi)

Yoshimitsu (1045-1127)

Yoshichika d. 1108

Yoshitada 1083-1109

Yoshikuni 1091-1155

Yoshioki

Yoshimune (Ishikawa)

Yoshinari Yoshikiyo Moriyoshi

Yoshinobu — Yoshinobu
Tameyoshi (1096-1156) — Tsunekuni
Yoshitoki — Yoshitaka
— Tadamune
— Yoshikiyo
— Yoshikatsu

Yoshishige (1135-1202)
Yoshiyasu d. 1157

Yoshizumi (Yamana)
Yoshitoshi (Satomi)
Yoshikane (Nitta)
Yoshisue (Tokugawa)
Yoshikiyo (Hosokawa)
Yoshikane (Ashikaga)

Masayoshi (Satake)
Katayoshi
Yoshisada
Yoshitsune (Yamamoto)
Kiyomitsu

Mitsunaga (Hemi)
Yoshinobu — Masayoshi (Takenouchi)
Nobuyoshi (Takeda) — Katanobu
Nagamitsu (Ogasawara) — Tomomasa (Hiraga)
Yoshisada (Yasuda) — Kagehira

Kotaka's Relationship to Takeda Shingen

ccording to a manuscript history of *Itto-ryu* that Kotaka Sadao wrote for his student, Tom Sovik, Kotaka's family was descended from the Takedas.[34]

Takeda Shingen's younger brother, Takeda Nobukado, (who very much resembled Shingen, so he played Shingen's double) had three sons. The second son, Takeda Nobutomo, inherited a fief in Hajikano (a county in Koshu) and became Jito (county administrator). Later, Takeda Shingen issued an order that the family name Takeda was allowed only to [be inherited by] the direct linage of Takeda Nobutora [Shingen's father]. In other words only the first son of every Takeda Clan derived from Takeda Nobutora was allowed to used the family name Takeda.

Takeda Nobutomo, thus, changed his name to Hajikano Genta-zaemon Mobutomo. He was one of [the famous] "24 generals of Takeda Shingen." [See painting on next page.] He also established a family rule that the first son [would] inherit the family name Hajikano, and the second son and so forth must change their name appropriately.

Thus, his second son was named Kotaka-kari (also pronounced Kotakari) Shogen Nobufumi. Nobufumi served as a general staff [officer] to Takeda Nobukado.

Kotaka-kari Shogen had three sons, with their respective family names [being] Kotaka-kari, Kotaka, and Takakari.

When Takeda Katsuyori [Shingen's son and heir] was defeated [at the famous Battle of Nagashino in 1575[34]], Kotaka-kari Shogen committed *harakiri* [along] with Takeda Katsuyori.

His [i.e., Kotaka-kari Shogen's] three sons were small children. [His eldest son] Kotaka-kari was exiled in Akao

---

* Kotaka *Sensei*'s English was not completely fluent. I have lightly edited his words for grammatical errors.

(currently Hyogo Prefecture [west of Kyoto and Osaka]) and his descendent became a chamberlain to Lord Akao. Kotaka and Takakari [were] exiled to Gongen-yama Mountains, the adjacent mountain range to the Daibosatsu Toge Mountains [west of Edo/Tokyo] and became *goshi* (landlord *samurai* [or farming *samurai*]).

It appears that Kotaka Sadao was a descendant of the Kotaka branch of descent, which would make him a direct, but distant descendant of Takeda Shingen.

Kotaka Sadao's Relationship to Takeda Shingen

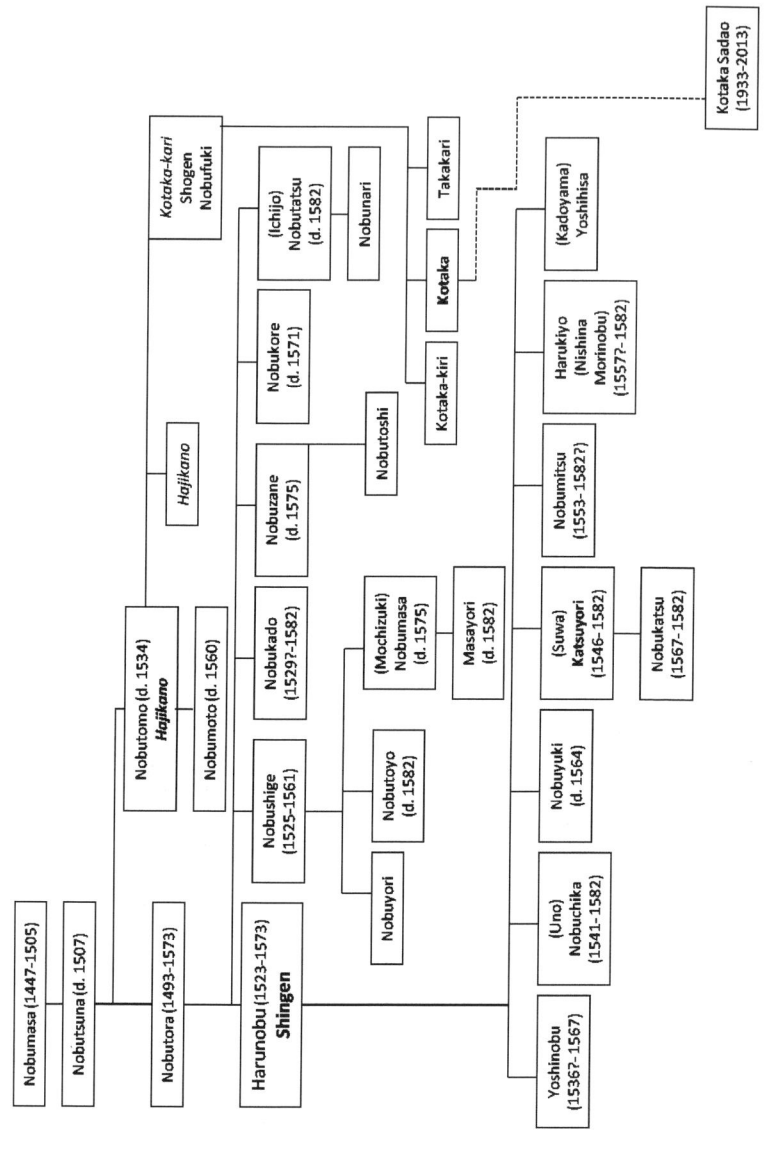

Partial list of Kotaka Sadao's early and senior students*

Among Kotaka *Sensei*'s earliest students who achieved black belt status were:

- The author, **Christopher M. Clarke,** Ph.D.[36]
- **Joe Doles,** DVM, veterinarian.

Among those who helped Kotaka *Sensei* open the Ohio State University club were:

- **David A. Diguangco**, who attended the Max M. Fisher College of Business at Ohio State from 1980-85 and the Air Force Institute of Technology at Wright-Patterson Air Force Base in Dayton, Ohio, during which time he trained with Kotaka and became one of his most senior students. He later attended the Defense Acquisition University at Fort Belvoir, Virginia before moving to Utah, where he has served in a variety of capacities as a program manager for the U.S. Air Force. He operated a *dojo* in Utah and was a key member of Kotaka's United States Classical Kendo Federation.[36] (See Appendix B, pages 161-164.)
- **Craig Campbell**. Craig, a senior practitioner of *Isshin-ryu karate*, began training with Kotaka in the late 1970s or early 1980s. Remaining in Columbus, Ohio as a professional martial arts instructor, he became Kotaka's right-hand man, frequent *uke* at clinics and demonstrations, the regular instructor at the Ohio State University club, and a frequent competitor in *kendo* competitions. He achieved the rank of 6th *dan*. Sadly, Craig passed away far too early at age 61 on February 9, 2014.[38]

Other senior students of Kotaka *Sensei* include:

- **Dr. Thomas Sovik,** professor of music theory and director

---

* Due to the shortage of records, the death of several key students, and my inability to contact others, this list is partial, provisional, and does not necessarily reflect accurately the seniority or rank of Kotaka's students. I have chosen in some cases not to list ranks due to the absence of information.

of Central European Studies and Exchanges and the College of Music, University of North Texas, Denton. Tom began training with Kotaka during the mid-1970s and was one step ahead of Craig Campbell in seniority, according to a personal communication. He trained with Kotaka while pursuing his Master's and Ph.D. degrees at Ohio State between 1975-1985. He achieved both *dan* ranking and permission to teach from Kotaka, and Kotaka *Sensei* was the best man at Tom's wedding.[39]

- **Larry Wilcoxen** was a student of Kotaka Sadao "one step junior to Craig Campbell," according to his friend, Tom Sovik. He continues to live in the Columbus, Ohio area and remains in touch with the Kotaka family.[40]

- **Dr. William "Bill" Dvorine** was a well-known dermatologist in the Baltimore-Washington, D.C. area and has been called the "father of *kendo* in the Mid-Atlantic region." Engaged in other martial arts, especially *Judo*, as a young man, he switched to *kendo* "as I got older to [do] something less injury-provoking." Dvorine apparently began to study *kendo* around 1970 with an exchange student from Japan. By 1975, he had established a *kendo* club in the Baltimore area. I have not been able to discover how he became associated with Kotaka. It appears that Dr. Kotaka was only one of many instructors Dr. Dvorine invited to teach at his school and that he was not, strictly speaking, a student of Kotaka or his *Kogen Itto-ryu*.[41]

- **Donald Yehling**, Ph.D. of central Ohio began training under Kotaka and Craig Campbell in 1985, according to his own account.[42] This apparently was while he was pursuing a Ph.D. in entomology and acarology (the study of mites and ticks). He was an instructor and research scientist at Ohio State and Ohio Dominican University, and a teacher at the Columbus Academy and the Columbus Torah Academy. Yehling trained directly with Kotaka for about 14 years, including hosting his club after Ohio State University made it virtually impossible for non-students to participate in on-campus activities. When Kotaka *Sensei* retired, he sanctioned Dr. Yehling to open his own school at teach the *Sakurai-ha Kogen Itto-ryu* curriculum.[43] Dr. Yehling died September 24, 2013.[43]

A few other people who achieved *dan* rank under Kotaka Sadao or his students include:

- **Patrick McTurner**, as of the mid– or late-1990s was listed as "Third Instructor" (under Kotaka and Campbell) at the Ohio State University Kendo/Iaido Club and ranked *Shoden* and *yodan* (1st level and 4th degree black belt).*

- **Keith Haney** in 1997 was listed as "Third Instructor" of the Weber State University Kendo Club under David Diguangco. He was ranked *Shoden* and *yodan* (1st level and 4th degree black belt.)

- **Christopher Watchman** as of 1997 was "Assistant Instructor" (*Shihan Dai*), *Kirigami*, and *nidan* (2nd degree). He apparently trained for several years with Kotaka *Sensei* before relocating to Idaho, where he seems to have continued his study under David Diguangco, reaching the rank of *sandan*.

- **Taro Swansen** reached *sandan* level and *mokuroku* under David Diguangco in Utah.

- **A.J. (Andrew) Bryant** trained with Kotaka from about 1995-1999, mostly in *iaido*. He does not claim qualification in Kotaka's style and, while continuing to practice the *iaido* he learned from him, apparently shifted his study to *Ono-ha Itto-ryu*.

- **Roger McPhail**, **Tony Saiki** and **Dave Bahde** reached the rank of *nidan* under David Diguangco.

- **John Mau, Marty Hing, Mike Wilkinson**, and **Andrea Wilkinson** all reached the rank of *shodan* under David Diguangco.

- **Jennifer Bowman, Nancy Griffith, Sarah Haddick,** and **Terry Lynn Wayne** all reached the rank of *nidan* under Tom Sovik at the All-Texas Christian Women's Kendo Federation.

- **Jane Bergman, Erica Cicanka, Donna Dewhurst, Margaret Hastings, Debbie Marshall, Tammy Shrone,** and **Leslie Steele** all reached the rank of *shodan* under Tom Sovik at the All-Texas Christian Women's Kendo Federation.

There are undoubtedly other students of *yudansha* rank of which I am not aware. I apologize for any and all omissions.

* On rankings and gradings, see Appendix F, below.

Top: Joe Doles around 1975 practicing *iaido* in Kotaka *Sensei*'s garage/*dojo*.

A class with Kotaka *Sensei* (back row, middle)
around 1975. The author is in the back row, left. Dr.
Joe Doles is in the back row, right. The
others are unidentified.

Kotaka Sadao's Students

David Diguangco
(top left)

Tom Sovik
(middle left)

Don Yehling
(right)

A young Craig
Campbell
(top, right)

Bill Dvorine
(middle, right)

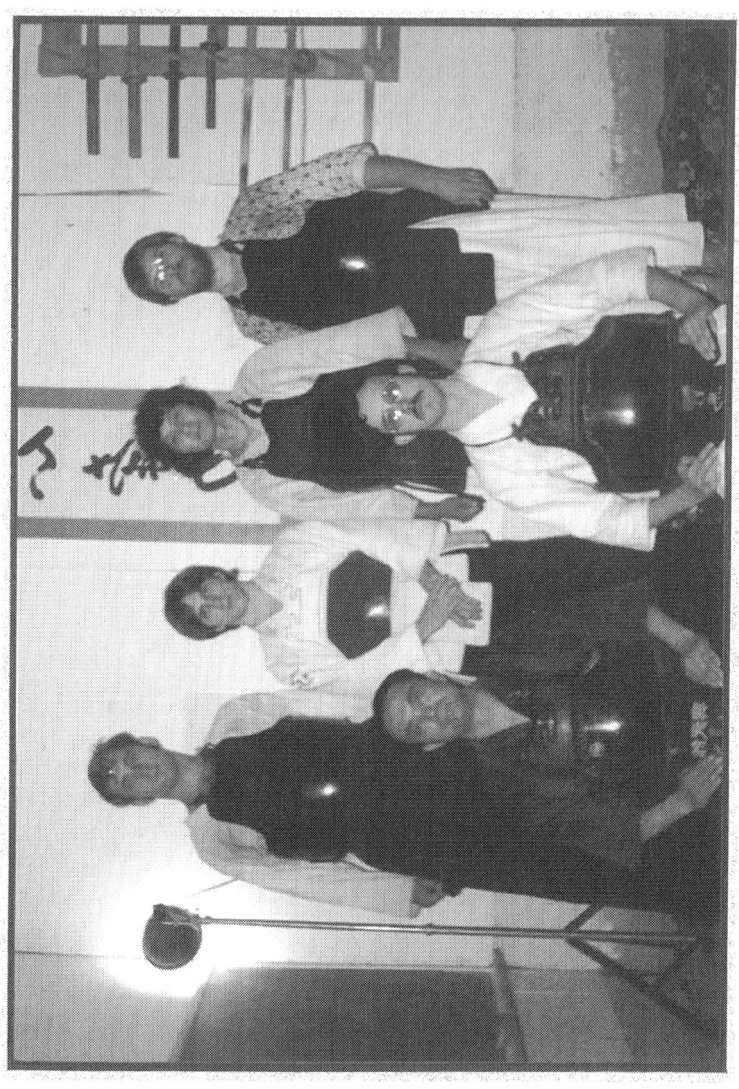

Front row, from left: Kurt Schmucker (guest), Kotaka *Sensei*.
Back row: Larry Wilcoxen, Craig Campbell Watanabe Mitsu, and Dr. Thomas
Sovik. Photo apparently from the mid– to late 1970s.

Schmucker as of about 2008 held ranks of *godan* in *Muso Shinden Ryu Iaido*,
yondan in *kendo*, *sandan* in *Shinto Muso Ryu Jodo*, and *shodan* in *Judo*. He
was an assistant instructor under Dr. William Dvorine in Maryland before
relocating to California. He is now a *godan* in *naginata* and vice president of
the US Naginata Federation.

Photo courtesy of Tom Sovik

44

Promotion of Dave Bahde (with certificate) to *nidan* by Dave Diguangco (right). Keith Haney (far left), Martin Hing (third from right), others unidentified.

Craig Campbell enthusiastically teaching *kendo* to youngsters.

The author and his students

Kenjutsu practice, Lake Winnipesaukee, NH August 1994.
Michael Pepe (*Joden*), author, James A True, Jr. (*Joden*), Jo McCulty,
Jules Pommier, Steven Tulimieri (*Joden*). (All ranks as of 2011.)

Tameshiwari, 2011. (L) Eric McLoney,
Okuiri.   (R) James A. True, Jr., *Joden.*
(Below) Jeanne McDonald and Kristen Pepe (both *Chuden*) performing
naginata kata.

The author in 2006 doing *Okuden Iai.* (Left: author; right: Steven Tulimieri).

The author in 2006 performing the application of *Okuden Iai Tsure dachi*
with senior students James A. True (left) and Steven Tulimieri,
both *Joden* rank.

Assessments of Kotaka Sadao's *Kendo* Ability

Various *kendo*-related web sites and discussion fora raised questions during the 1990s and the first decade of the century about Kotaka *Sensei*'s *bona fides*. Many of these questions came from people who did not know him; some cannot be answered. There are some anomalies that are puzzling, including his statements at various times about his rank and title, the connection of his "*Sakurai-ha Kogen Itto-ryu*" to the recognized *Kogen Itto-ryu* style of the Henmi family, and the relationship of his teacher to both the *Kogen Itto-ryu* and the Shinsengumi. Kotaka's claims to success in competition have also raised questions, in part because most of them rest on his word and have not been (or cannot be) subject to verification.

Rank. When I first met Kotaka *Sensei* in the early 1970s, he wrote down for me that he had received the *chuden* level from Sakurai *Sensei* before the latter's death in 1954. He wrote that this was equivalent to 4th *dan*.[44] During his period of training in California, he was promoted to 5th *dan* in *iaido* and later to 6th *dan* in *kendo*, and was a member of the U.S. Kendo Federation.[45] His word and membership were well enough respected and recognized that he was able to recommend me for *shodan* rank, which the Federation issued.

In later statements, however, he purportedly said he held a 7th *dan, okuden* (senior or inductee to the "hidden" or "secret" levels of the style), and *menkyo* in *Kogen Itto-ryu* and the status of *hanshi*.[46] It is not clear what organization awarded these ranks or titles, and it relatively unusual for a 7th *dan* to be given the title of *hanshi*. At various times, Kotaka *Sensei* reported his *judo* rank as *sandan* and *yodan*.

Competition. Kotaka's claims to success in competition have also raised questions, in part because most of them rest on his word and have not been subject to verification. While I was still training with *Sensei*, for example, he told me that he had recently visited Canada, where he (as a *godan*) had taken on three 7th *dan kenshi* who were visiting from Japan and

48

had decisively defeated all three. In a 1997 interview with Dr. Phil Fellman, a black belt in *Hokushin Itto-ryu* and *Kameyama-ha Owari Yagyu-ryu* and an expert on Japanese swords, Kotaka *Sensei* said:

PVF [Philip V. Fellman]: David [Diguangco] also mentioned that you recently attended a special tournament in Tokyo where you fought and defeated fifty *kendoka* ranked *nanadan* [7th *dan*] and above in a row.

KS [Kotaka Sadao]: Yes, this was the joint practice of the Tokyo Police Department and Osaka Police Department Kendo Clubs. They have an advanced group which requires 7th *dan* for membership. Both Tokyo and Osaka Police Departments have excellent *kendo*. Their *kendo* is much stronger than any college *kendo*. College *kendo* and college *judo* simply cannot handle police *kendo* and *judo*. The one exception to this, I find to be Waseda University in Japan. I feel a strong kinship with the Waseda team.

PVF: Yes, I am familiar with this school, Yamaoka [Tesshu] *sensei* spent a short time on the Keio University Kendo team, which was their rival.

KS: In Waseda University, Sasamori Jinzaburo *Sensei* is using *Ono-ha Itto-Ryu* style, very much the same *Ono-ha Itto-Ryu* style used by the Tokyo and Osaka Police Department teams, which has a very strong attack. I believe that these are the finest martial artists in Japan today (the Tokyo and Osaka Police teams members).

PVF: But nonetheless they were not able to score *ippon*?

KS: Only Kato *sensei* was able to score clear *ai-uchi* [strike at the same time].

PVF: What about *kendo* in the United States?

KS: Hayashi Tatsuo *sensei* of the University of Michigan comes here to Columbus to practice with us, and we very much respect and enjoy his participation. As a college student, he was the Captain of the Waseda Kendo team since his sophomore year. I believe he was also 1st place champion at some point in an All American Kendo Championship. After he came here to Columbus and could not score *ippon*,

49

he became more interested in classical Kendo and renewed his studies in Japan. We always enjoy his visits.[47]

These incidents would have occurred when Kotaka was around 60 years of age. While to many this may seem a "tall tale," my own experience with Kotaka *Sensei* was that he was all but untouchable. I was not the only one to hold that opinion. During the same interview, Dr. Fellman, an experienced practitioner in two styles of *kendo* had this to say after crossing swords with Kotaka:

> PVF: I noticed from my own match with you that you are able to anticipate virtually any attack before it arrives. I recall quite well that even as I moved only mentally, or simply prepared my breathing, you changed *maai*, negating my attack before even the first physical movement was begun.[48]

Another (unidentified) *kendo* practitioner, apparently a student of Kotaka, posted the following comment on a *kendo* forum in 2003:

> I wouldn't rely on age as the main reason as to why they [8th *dan kenshi*] don't compete. I agree with others when they say that they have moved on to a higher level. For example, Kotaka *sensei* is 67 years old and looks like a feeble old man. Lee *sensei* who is not older than 35 and has won championship in Korea and is incredibly fast but still cannot best Kotaka *sensei*. Although my *sensei* has been doing *kendo* for 60 years could be a factor. But what I'm trying to get across is that when they fence, Kotaka *sensei* doesn't move until the opponent has moved and then it is too late for the opponent. Lee *sensei* practices modern *kendo*, Kotaka *sensei* practices classical *kendo*, maybe this also has something to do with it.[49]

In an article written after his interview with Dr. Kotaka, Dr. Fellman wrote:

> I found Dr. Kotaka to be a charming, humble, knowledgeable gentleman of the old school, and he spent a good deal of time both inspecting my *shinken* [real sword] and allowing me to thoroughly examine his own sword… [After some *iaido* practice] we put away the *shinken* and engaged in a little

shinai dueling, with Kotaka *sensei* supervising. I think that at first, Yamaoka *sensei's* technique was a bit foreign to them. I quickly found that when I tried to use *Hokushin Itto-Ryu* techniques, I was immediately overpowered by the much stronger *Kohgen Itto-Ryu* style. In that regard, I was greatly impressed that among "strong" or "hard" styles of *kenjutsu*, no system which I have seen has more vigor than *Kohgen Itto Ryu*, which even in [the] Edo period had a very powerful reputation.

Kotaka *sensei* explained this as a "one blow, one kill" style, and described how such vigorous and deadly techniques had been necessary to control the lawless *ronin* in pre-Meiji Kyoto who often made their living through extorting merchants and through other criminal activities. These *ronin* were quite beyond the abilities of the police to handle, and battles with the *Shinsen Gumi* often left the gutters of Kyoto literally running with blood.

Finding that my *Hokushin* techniques were completely inadequate, I then switched to the softer, more fluid Yagyu techniques, which we had inherited from Kameyama *sensei* and focused more upon smaller movements and attacks to *kote...*

In a series of amusing exchanges, David [Diguangco] kept charging me long after he had been decapitated [*sic.*], so much so that at one point, Craig [Campbell] had to tell him, "David you can't keep swinging at him after your arms have been cut off."

Once we switched to full contact fencing in *bogu*, this situation was soon reversed. There, I went from being the aggressor to being the punching bag, and David got his revenge by scoring repeated and powerful *men* that left my ears ringing. This time, his enthusiasm was reversed and he was banging away at me after I was surely quite dead.

Finally, Dr. Kotaka put an end to my torment, and engaged me in a more familiar duel-like confrontation (although we still wore *bogu*). I think I can safely say that never have I faced a more skilled or a more sensitive, and spiritually attuned opponent. Knowing discretion to be the better part of valor, rather than attacking, I simply spent all my time (about twenty minutes) probing in vain for an opening in Kotaka *sensei's* defense.

While he presented me with several apparent openings, I knew that to take any of them would mean instant defeat. Kotaka *sensei* has a sensitivity which must be felt to be understood. If I used internal breathing to expand my zone of control (a kind of *seme* technique) he simply stepped back, negating the attack. As far as physical adjustments went, I found that he could adjust to any change in *Kamae* [stance], no matter how rapid or how complex without leaving me the slightest edge or beat for an opening. Most astonishing was the fact that he could see the attack forming in my mind, when it was still just the faintest glimmer of an idea. I feel that in over twenty years of studying martial arts, much of it internal styles, I have never seen a more spiritually developed instructor than Dr. Kotaka.

Throughout this prolonged dance, Kotaka *sensei's zanshin* [mental focus] never wavered in the slightest, try though I might to break it. Subjectively, it felt as if the two of us were trapped inside a tunnel with an opening big enough to let only one of us out. I felt very much like a character in an Eric Lustbader novel, standing on the "killing ground", only it was impossible to make any headway against Kotaka *sensei's* immovable will. Finally after more than twenty minutes of this, Kotaka *sensei* suggested that we just try some normal *kendo* passes to share and exchange techniques, which was a great relief to me. Unlike David and Craig, he did not take this opportunity to pound me into a pulp (which he surely could have done) but rather used it in a non-competitive instructional way to show me many of the *Kohgen Itto-Ryu* and Classical Kendo techniques and how they could be applied in different situations.[50]

Kotaka Sadao's Account of his "*Dojo* Breaking" in Japan

There is a very old tradition in Japan of going on *musha shugyo* (traveling study and practice) during which a swordsman would look for various *kenjutsu dojo* and masters and issue challenges. If the students, or instructor, in a school beat the challenger, he would either slink away in disgrace or stay on to learn and master the new style. These bouts were conducted with either *bokken* (wooden swords) or *shinken* (real swords), and injuries or deaths were common. This tradition was eventually banned in the early 1600s by the Tokugawa shogunate, but continued nonetheless. It continues today, although in a much more "civilized" form: a *kenshi* might seek or be issued an invitation to another school, at which he would size himself up against the best students in the school, competing in modern *kendo* with *bogu*, a referee and standard rules. This is sometimes called *dojo yaburi* (道場破り).

Below, Kotaka Sadao recounts in his own words (lightly edited to improve his English) one successful competition against two very high-ranking *kenshi* in 1986 and a "*dojo* breaking" incident he participated in in 1989. He was reticent to "brag" about such incidents, but wrote about them privately to his student and friend, Dr. Tom Sovik. Somehow word of Kotaka *Sensei*'s matches got out and drew considerable skepticism on various *kendo* web forums. The details he includes suggest his veracity.

First is his account of competing against two very highly ranked visitors from Japan from a letter to Dr. Tom Sovik in May 1986:

> I can not explain well this spiritual state of mind. This might be the state of mind that my *sensei* used to talk about. I felt this spiritual change when I practiced with you in the *Yosei-kan Dojo*, Covington.* I felt a marked change in my *iaido* and *shinai keiko*. Right after you left Columbus, I was invited to [the] Chicago *Dojo* to have an exhibition match

---

* Kotaka, already a very talented and formidable swordsman, reported having an enlightening experience while practicing with Dr. Tom Sovik at the *karate dojo* of *Hanshi* William Dometrich, a high-level teacher of *Chito-ryu* style. Dometrich often hosted visiting Japanese and Okinawans and became close friends with Nagamine Takayoshi (1945-2012), inheritor as *soke* of the *Matsubayashi (Shorin-ryu) karate* system, who spent several years in college nearby.

with two *kendo sensei* from Japan, named Matsumoto *Sensei* and Okuzono *Sensei*. Matsumoto sensei was 7th *dan* ([he now] is 8th *dan*), the chief *kendo* instructor of [the] Tokyo Metropolitan Police Force, and four times grand champion of [the] Annual All Japan Police Force *Kendo* Tournament. He was ([and] still is) the champion of the Eastern Region Police Force Kendo Federation. Okuzono *Sensei* is the counterpart of Matsumoto *Sensei*. He is 7th dan ([he now] is also 8th *dan**), the chief instructor of the Osaka Metropolitan Police Force, and the champion of the Western Region Police Force *Kendo* Federation. The two *sensei* have been the finalists for the Grand Championship Match of the All Japan Police Force Kendo Tournament for many years.

I had an exhibition match with Matsumoto *Sensei* in the first day and with Okuzono *Sensei* on the second day. Fortunately, I got three points each from both *sensei*.

I have not disclosed this [to] anyone before. This sounds like bragging. What I want to tell you is that the mental state or spiritual enlightenment that I acquired in the Covington *Dojo* by practicing with you helped me to play *kendo* beyond my expectation. I got some confidence that no matter how strong an opponent is, I never get beaten up very badly. I can counter the opponent at least draw, if not a total victory.

Following is his own account of his "*dojo* breaking" experience in Japan in March 1989:

The trip was a half business and a half vacation... I could squeeze out times to practice *kendo* in three major *dojos* in Tokyo and two in Gunma Prefecture. All the *dojos* are headed by *Ono-ha Itto-ryu*-oriented 8th *dan* or 9th *dan sensei*s whom I had exhibition matches in San Francisco, Chicago, and/or New York in the past years.

The membership of these dojos is restricted to 5th *dan* through 7th *dan* holders who are also teaching *kendo* in police forces, police academies, universities, and colleges in Tokyo and

---

* Achieving 8th *dan* in *kendo* is notoriously difficult. It is the highest grade awarded through testing (9th and 10th *dan* are awarded for contributions to *kendo*). The reported pass rate of 7th *dan*s testing for 8th *dan* is less than one-percent. At least one modern man took the test 24 years in a row up to the age of 78 without passing.

Gunma. In other words, they are professional *samurais*. These *dojos* are regarded as training centers for champion class *kendoists* for preparing national and international *kendo* tournaments and high ranking *dan* promotion examinations.

I was honored to sit in the chief instructor's seating place of all the above-mentioned *dojos*. What this meant is that I must stay in the *keiko* [practice] against all the members of the host *dojo* one after another, or until the *keiko* is over, without resting, especially without taking off *men* [face and head protector]. If one takes off his or her *men* during a *keiko* session, it is called "*kabuto-wo-nugu*" (taking off the war helmet = surrender to the enemy). To stay on a *keiko* session without taking off one's *men* is called *uchi-kiri* (hitting through (enemy line) all the way) or *kiri-tohshi* [ed.: possibly *kiri-otoshi*] (cutting through (enemy line) all the way). If I would have to take off my *men* and take a rest to catch up my breath or to drink water, I would lose my chief instructor's seating place they offered me in the beginning. Someone next to me (usually the chief instructor of the host *dojo*) would close up or retake the chief instructor's seating place. Thus, when the *keiko* session is over, I would have to move to the lowest seating place. Even if I stay on the *keiko* all the way through, at the end of the *keiko* session I must have an exhibition match with the chief *sensei* or the highest ranking (or strongest) member(s) of the host *dojo*, as many opponents as the host *dojo* people request, in front of all the *dojo* members and visitors who serve as referees. If I loose this exhibition match by self-recognition or judge without words by referees (spectators), I must sit in the seating place lower than that of the winner.

Fortunately, I made *kiri-toshi* in all the *dojos* and won all the exhibition matches by scoring uncontested *ippons*. So, I was able to keep my highest seating place in all the *dojos* I visited. This is called "*dojo yaburi*" (breaking *dojo*). I am very pleased with the outcome, because this proves that our *Sakurai-ha Kogen Itto-ryu kendo* is superior over *Ono-ha Itto-ryu*... Now I can call myself as a successor of Sakurai Gen'noshin Fumitaka *Sensei* with confidence, because I am able to defend my *dojo* from any or all the *dojo yaburi* as Sakurai *Sensei* did.

Personal Recollections of Kotaka Sadao

The Author's Personal Recollections

I was one of Kotaka *Sensei's* earliest students after he moved from California to Columbus, Ohio in the early 1970s. I first met him when he performed a demonstration of *iaido* at a local *karate* tournament, to the best of my recollection, in about 1972-73. Although most of the audience seemed bored with the slow and dignified performance, expecting to see something more akin to Bruce Lee with a sword, as a *yodan* in *karate* and fairly well experienced in Okinawan *kobudo* (weaponry), I could see immediately that he was the "real deal" and that I had to find a way to train with him. Altogether, I trained with him for about 5-6 years in his garage long before he opened a club at the Ohio State University and before any of his later students, who were to open schools and gain high rank under him, had appeared.

During the entire time I trained with him, there were only a few other regular students, Joe Doles (who became a veterinarian and moved to the Cleveland area), a Japanese, and a Taiwan-born Chinese, who spoke Japanese because he had grown up on Taiwan during the Japanese occupation. Neither trained consistently, and I was often the only student to show up.

Sensei and I would often spend three hours or more working out together, usually doing about an hour of *iaido*— the *Omori-ryu seiza-no-bu* and the *Hasegawa Eishin-ryu hiza-no-bu*—before donning our *bogu* and "sparring" for an hour, an hour-and-a-half, or two hours without stopping. Later we added the *Nihon Kendo no Kata*, the official two-person form of the Japanese *kendo* federation. The only breaks we took were to change equipment.

As a young and enthusiastic trainee, I regularly ran three to six miles a day, lifted weights five to six days a week, played hours of racket ball every day, and practiced *karate* every evening. So it came as a total surprise to me that a man nearly twice my age (he would have been in his 40s, and I in my 20s) could leave me totally exhausted at the end of each workout while he hardly broke a sweat or breathed hard. And he didn't play the kinds of tricks many *sensei* do, making the students do endless repetitions of basic techniques and exercises while saving their energy for *keiko*. What I did, he did.

His conditioning amazed me, and it was quite some time before I realized that it was less a latter of conditioning than of perfect timing and effective execution. With *sensei* there was no wasted movement. Likewise, he astounded me with his flexibility and leg/hip strength. There was a table, about waist high, in the corner of his garage/*dojo* over which he had placed hooks on which to hang the *bogu* between training sessions. Numerous times I watched *sensei* place one foot on this table and step up with the other foot, all the while holding a set of *bogu*, and never assisting himself with the other hand. It was a feat that in my wildest imagination—and with at least several inches of height advantage—I could never have duplicated.

Despite the *koubushi* ("mouth warriors") who have questioned his *bona fides*, I can attest to the extremely high quality of *sensei's* martial ability. During *keiko*, he was simply so efficient that he ran me ragged trying to find an opening, then pounced with a devastating and quick strike. His perception was inerrant; I don't think that in 5-6 years of training with

him I ever scored a clean point on him. And I well remember the many times he evaded my *men* strike, only to feel the "thwack" of his *shinai* across my *do*, as he reappeared as if by magic to my side, almost behind me. (This technique was one of the specialties of his *Kogen Itto-ryu*.)

Several times we had visitors, including some very competitive young *yudansha* from Japan. He simply made them look silly, playing with them like children. But he was always polite and encouraging in doing so, a real gentleman. His skill in *iaido* and *shinai kendo* was simply unsurpassed in my experience.

Whatever doubts or questions some people may have had about his claim to teach "*Kogen Itto-ryu*," no one could dispute the quality of his martial ability.

Kotaka *Sensei* teaching.

Source: the now-defunct website of the United States Classical Kendo Federation.

Personal Recollections of Dr. Thomas Sovik

The Worst Student of the Sakurai-ha Kogen Ittō-ryū Remembers His Teacher

Dr. Thomas Sovík had the privilege of studying directly under Kotaka Sadao, *shodai sōke* of the *Sakurai-ha Kogen Ittō-ryū* and headmaster of the United States Classical *Kendō* Federation. He holds the rank of *godan* with *renshi menkyo* and sits as advisor to the All-Texas Christian Women's *Kendō* Federation. He currently serves as Professor of Music Theory and Director of Central European Studies & Exchanges at the University of North Texas, residing in Fort Worth with his wife and children.

Now, at the passing of Kotaka Sukesaburo (Minamotono) Sadayasu Sadao, Dr. Sovik provides us with an intimate portrait of a revered teacher in the *Kogen Ittō-ryū* and a glimpse of what training was like in the Kotaka *dōjō*.

* * *

Introduction

The typical new face in the *dōjō*, sporting a white belt that's as stiff as a two-by-four, dreams of the day when he'll wear a black belt; when he does earn that black belt, his ego will lead him to fantasies of going even further, of becoming an Olympic *jūdōka*, a *karate* master with a lucrative chain of martial-art studios, or a Jedi-trained *kendō* master.

If you're senior, you've been to that place, and (hopefully) you've outgrown the silliness. And, if you're senior, you've come to appreciate what life was like as a white belt. No one yells at a white belt, you're not expected to know anything, and you're free from all commitment. Your only responsibility is to show up and attempt to learn something, and even *that* is optional. (Bill Lovret would tell the story of how, during a *yudansha* class, he became angry and asked how many of them wanted to go back to wearing a white belt; much to his chagrin, there was no shortage of volunteers!)

When you become senior, you've moved beyond sport and game; you understand that what you teach on the *dōjō* floor must be perfect, or not at all. When you become senior, your words carry a degree of gravitas. Smart people know that old people have something to teach them.

When Chris Clarke asked me to contribute to this memorial volume honoring Kotaka Sukesaburo (Minamotono) Sadayasu Sadao (1933-2013), I procrastinated out of a profound sadness. I was senior in Kotaka *Sensei's dōjō* for a decade and then entwined in an old-school master-apprentice relationship for yet another decade. He was the best man at my wedding. He promoted me to the rank of *godan* (the rank he held when I first began training with him) and entrusted me with the *renshi menkyo* (teaching license). When he thought that I finally knew enough to lead my own *dōjō*, he was there for me as master, friend, and confidant.

As I look back over the last 40 years, I'm reminded of the moment in the *Seven Samurai* when Kambei Shimada, leader of the group, reflects on how much time has passed in their lives, what they have sacrificed as *samurai*, and how parents and friends have long since died. They are alone in the world.

Today, my *kendō sensei*, Kotaka Sadao, is dead. Bill Dvorine, who preceded me as a student of Kotaka *Sensei*—is likewise dead. Craig Campbell, to whom I was senior by a single lesson and then who succeeded me as senior when I moved across the United States to become a university professor— dead. Don Yehling, who succeeded Craig as senior in the *dōjō*—dead.

Many of us in the Kotaka *dōjō* also trained in *mengei* (peasant arts) with well-known teachers, going beyond *kendō* to deepen our understanding of our primary martial art. Jay T. Will, the well-known full-contact fighter and referee in the 1970s and 80s who brought me to *dan* ranking in the *Kosho-ryū*—is likewise dead. Bill Dometrich, head of the *Chito-ryū karate* in the United States with whom I had studied briefly— dead. Bill Sosa, with whom I had studied *aikidō*—dead.

Fortunately, David Diguangco, who was promoted to *rokudan* by Kotaka *Sensei* in 2000, is still very much alive and active as headmaster of the Ogden *Kendō* Club in Ogden, Utah. Diguangco *Sensei* and I appear to be the last men standing, waiting to see which of us will be the one to turn out the lights and lock the door in the lineage of senior *yudansha* who studied the *Sakurai-ha Kogen Ittō-ryū* directly from its *sōke*. I wish him the best of health and good fortune, as I am ill-equipped— having been run over by a drunk driver (literally)—to step easily into that lead position. It is David who now carries the heavy responsibility of preserving the *ryū-ha* as it was taught by Dr. Kotaka.

Kotaka *Sensei* was, in every respect, a classical Japanese *samurai* who had been uncomfortably displaced 400 years into the future. He was a fencing master who could trace his lineage back to Itō Ittōsai Kagehisa (1560–1653?), founder of the *Ittō-ryū* (one of the three major sword styles of feudal Japan). Kotaka studied directly under Sakurai Gen'noshin Muneyoshi, the great grandson of Tsukue Gen'noshin Humitaka ("Ryunosuke Tsukue," the protagonist of the *samurai*-novel *Diabosatsu Tōge*—which remains the second-longest book in the Japanese language, with 1533 chapters in 41 volumes).

After coming to the United States and becoming disappointed to see that much of U.S. *kendō* had become "sport" kendō, Dr. Kotaka founded the United States Classical *Kendō* Federation. It was his wish that the *Sakurai-ha Kogen Ittō-ryū* would remain a *combat* discipline. In this, he was absolutely steadfast. Modern *kendō*, in his opinion, had become little more than a frenetic party game in which one hacked his opponent to death with a series of paper cuts.

To some, Dr. Kotaka was an anachronism who had outlived his time and purpose; to me, he was both a merciless teacher living in an era that had long since passed and a patient and loving step-father who gave me much beyond what I could have ever imagined.

I owe this gentleman a debt that I can never repay.

1. A Relationship of Military Professionals

I thought that my father, who passed away on Thanksgiving morning 2013 at the age of 93, and Kotaka *Sensei* would have had an awkward relationship.

After fierce campaigns at both Guadalcanal and on Cape Gloucester, my father survived one of the bloodiest campaigns in the history of the U.S. Marine Corps, and the bloodiest battle within that campaign, on Peleliu.

After his 235-man unit, K Company of the 3rd Battalion, 1st Marines, captured "The Point" (Umurbrogol Mountain, which overlooked the airfield and which contained 500 heavily fortified limestone caves and bunkers connected by tunnels), the Marines were surrounded by Japanese troops under the command of Colonel Nakagawa Kunio. During the next 30 hours, K Company—out of both ammunition and water—repulsed repeated attacks. When the battle was over, only 78 Marines remained alive, and only 18 men were still standing to defend The Point.

My father was one of those 18 Marines—nearly every one of them wounded—left standing after a battle that had degenerated to vicious hand-to-hand combat with knives, shovels, empty ammunition boxes, fists, and pieces of coral. My father then went on teach to hand-to-hand combat as a Drill Instructor at Parris Island.

Although he would never speak of it, my father carried the scars of Guadalcanal, of Cape Gloucester, and particularly of those 30 hours on Peleliu until he passed. On his deathbed in the moments before he passed, he cried out to God—over and over—to forgive him for the "monster" he had become and for the things he did during that last battle.

And yet when these men spoke—after my father had experienced the horrors of the Pacific and after Kotaka *Sensei* (a bit younger than my father) had experienced the horrors unleashed on the Japanese mainland—they spoke as professional soldiers. Neither harbored any animosity toward the other; each acknowledged that the many who had died, and those who did what had to be done, were professionals carrying out their duty.

2. The "Legitimate" Martial-Art Instructor

Today, if you want to run a martial-art school in America, the first step is buy a big building (air conditioning is a must-have)—so that you can "look like a duck." Then, you have to "walk like a duck." In fact, there are more 10th-degree black belts and heads of international martial-art organizations on my block today than there were worldwide when I began training.

As for training with a lowly 5th-degree black belt in his garage? What nonsense! Most Americans, with a four-minute attention span and an understanding of the martial arts that was spawned by the *Green Hornet* and Kung-fu cartoons, would have written this guy off as a charlatan.

Could Dr. Kotaka have afforded a "real" *dōjō* instead of a farm shed? Absolutely. He could have easily written a check. He was a chemist-engineer working for the Battelle Corporation, a global research and development organization dedicated to the development of new technologies, the commercialization of new products, and management of U.S. government research projects.

It's not that they were paying him minimum wage. He just didn't accept that he had to "buy" his credentials with a big building and a fancy title.

Postscript: In my *dōjō*—which also happens to be in my garage—there is a photograph of the *Yokukan Dōjō* at the Hen'mi family home (it was Hen'mi Tashiro Yoshitoski who founded our substyle of the *Ittō-ryū*), in Saitama Prefecture. This is the *hombu* (headquarters) *dōjō* of the *Kogen Ittō-ryū*. It's a farm shed. The space is about 50 feet long and 15 feet wide, and farm stuff is still stored inside the building. Whatever free space is available is used for martial-art training.

3. What Kind of *Dōjō* Is This?

I've often wondered what it would have been like to train in a (normal) *kendō dōjō*, as I suspect ours fell pretty far from the tree. By definition, we were a *kendō dōjō*—we had *bōgu* (*kendō* armor), *shinai* (bamboo practice sword), and *hakama*; we practiced the same basic forms, and we beat one another with sticks. But while other *kendō-ka* played by points and rules, trained on a well-defined hardwood chessboard, and had an affiliation (with the United States *Kendō* Federation), "our" little wooden universe harkened back to the 16th century.

While other *dōjō* practiced "sport *kendō*," Kotaka *Sensei* was teaching a *koryū* (a traditional Japanese martial art that predates the Meiji Restoration in 1868).

While other *dōjō* limited attacks to the *men, dō,* and *kote*, we were allowed to use the dangerous *tsuki* to the throat and stomach. There was nothing quite like running at full speed toward your opponent only to be stopped by a *shinai* rammed into your 3x5-inch throat protector (and hopefully that *shinai* didn't slip to either side, because that *shinai* would have gone through your throat), which then caused your head to rock backward as the rest of the mass moved forward. As your feet went into mid-air, the back of your skull slammed into the hardwood floor.

Whacking your attacker on the back of the head, which was not protected by the *men* and which was forbidden in sport *kendō*, was never considered a transgression in the Kotaka *dōjō*. We learned quickly never to turn our back on an opponent!

If you splintered or dropped your *shinai*, you reverted to *jūdō, karate, aikidō* or to just plain muscle and ingenuity. Artificial "points" didn't matter; the match wasn't over until one student ripped the helmet off the head of his opponent. Considering that the *men* is tightly secured with *himo* (cords) to protect the *kendō-ka*'s face and head, it's not difficult to imagine how our already-less-than-handsome faces looked after a four-hour practice—scarred, swollen, and black-and-blue.

We drilled incessantly with the short, heavyweight *bokken* of the *Ittō-ryū* while wearing the *onigote* ("devil's gloves"), thick padded mittens the size of raccoons that allowed for full contact on the *kote*—or resulted in a broken forearm if the *shidachi* (junior student) missed the *onigote*. Fortunately, the injury happened only once during my tenure in the Kotaka *dōjō*.

We trained with the *shinken* (real sword), the *aikuchi* (dagger), and the *motsushaku* (solid wooden fan), and we were expected to fend off attacks with the *bō* (staff), *naginata* (halberd), and *yari* (spear).

While other *kendō-ka* had a *dōjō*, the world was our practice field—much in the spirit of Ittō Ittōsai (the founder of the *Ittō-ryū*, who himself never had a physical *dōjō*). We trained in the close quarters of *Sensei*'s garage, practicing *hosshato* (techniques for fighting multiple opponents in a darkened room); on hot summer evenings, we trained in his backyard and drank the warm fluid that trickled out of a black, moldy garden hose; barefoot, we practiced the *bokken-gata* on an asphalt rooftop (mercifully, he cut that practice short because all of us had large burn-blisters on our feet, and we never repeated that experiment); we practiced the classical version of "mixed martial-arts" (*Ittō-ryū kendō* combined with *Daitō-ryū aikijūjutsu*) with snow swirling around our bare feet and into the *hakama* through the *soba* (side panels), freezing our asses.

On the darkest of nights, in both summer and winter, we would train in the yard. This was an exercise that focused our training. Distance and awareness had to be perfect; we were, after all, training with live blades.

There was something primal, spiritual, and utterly spectacular about practicing outdoors! With the summer wind blowing across the full of our body, we would wield *katana* and *naginata* under a sky illuminated by billions of stars. With teeth chattering in the autumn rain or mid-winter snow, we would glide across slippery grass. When lightning flashed to a thunderous peal of thunder, ghost-white faces flickered in the darkness, only to fade to blackness in an instant.

I fear that we're losing our connection both to the founders and to the world in which they developed their particular arts. We still practice the movements, but we've made the whole thing plastic, commercial, easy, an "air-conditioned sport"—tennis on Tuesday, *kendō* on Wednesday, yoga on the weekend.

Training in the Kotaka *dōjō*, while severe, fostered a camaraderie within the group that, between some of the members, survived three and four decades after those people had moved on to living real lives.

4. Promotion Exams

I was never overly preoccupied with rank. I already held *dan* ranking in the *Kosho-ryū* and was making a (small) name for myself on the tournament circuit—not because I had any real skill, but simply because I loved to hit and loved being hit. My first lesson with Dr. Kotaka, in the garage of someone with whom I could barely communicate, was just a lark . . . which ended up to be life.

It never occurred to me that we weren't having promotion exams. With Kotaka *Sensei*, it was "Every day is a promotion exam." Because Kotaka *Sensei* never had a *dōjō* of more than a handful of students at any one time (because those who wanted to "pay for lessons" rather than making the commitment soon absented themselves from the *dōjō*), there was no need to line us up to jump through a list of hoops.

He could teach a monkey how to swing a *shinai* in weekly lessons. He needed the time with us at the kitchen table and in his study to teach us how to be *more* than just someone who could swing a *shinai*. It was the little things that now seem to have been his most important lessons.

It's fairly well known in the industry that Japanese instructors tend to be gentle and polite with students they think are hopeless; these students merely help pay the rent and make training affordable for the serious students. Kotaka *Sensei* was always gentle and polite with us, so we naturally assumed that we were bozos. On the other hand, we told ourselves that if *Sensei* was making the effort to spend time with us and to gently correct our behavior, it meant that we were *his* bozos, and that there was a faint hope that we might—eventually—become serious students.

He once explained it to me, drawing an analogy to church. He could preach "do what I say" to a congregation of a thousand, or he could preach "do what I do" to a handful of apostles. To him, it wasn't what you preached on Sunday that was important; rather, it was the example by which you lived.

Ill-mannered, bumbling, and unappreciative students though we were, there was an intimacy in training that only a few (see Dave Lowry's *Autumn Lightning: The Education of an American Samurai,* 1985) have the opportunity to experience. Once again, Bill Lovret (a funny guy with a wry sense of humor), in his *The Way and the Power: Secrets of Japanese Strategy* (1987), had it absolutely right. It wasn't that these people are faster or stronger, or better or worse. They're just different.

5. Get that Dog Off of the Couch!

As senior in the *dōjō,* I had the singular privilege of accompanying Kotaka *Sensei* on numerous occasions as he traveled to give demonstrations and seminars and to accept invitations to teach at particular *dōjō.* In his *It's a Lot Like Dancing: An Aikidō Journey* (1993), Terry Dobson, traveling as *uchideshi* (senior disciple) to Morihei Ueshiba, gives us a wonderful picture of what was expected of the senior student on these adventures. And, in fact, my experience was pretty close to that which Terry portrayed as his own.

I would make the arrangements, handle the paperwork, carry the bags and *bōgu* as well as everything else, and get us checked into the motel. I'd draw Dr. Kotaka's bath and then be on hand in case he might slip and fall; I'd have his red, plastic flip-flops ready to go at the edge of the tub and be holding the towel to drape across his shoulders. I would then take the extra pillow and blanket out of the closet and sleep on the floor beside the single king-size bed in case my *sensei* would need something. In the morning, I would rise before the alarm clock would sound (sons of Marines know that drinking x amount of water will cause you to wake up in x amount of time in order to pee), quietly shower, and then run down to the lobby to have his coffee on the nightstand.

When I would return home from these demonstrations and seminars, the skin would have been beaten off of my knuckles, my forearms would look like rolled-up wet copies of the *New York Times*, and there would be a mass of welted purple flesh under my left underarm. And then, the next weekend, we'd repeat the process.

How many fast-food Americans, who've grown up on a diet of entitlement, would tolerate this type of "instructor abuse"? No beginner, however willing and impressionable he may be, would put up with it; no junior *yudansha*, impressed with his place in the hierarchy, would see this type of servility as compatible with his station.

For me, this was no fantasy world of following Obiwan Kenobi through the galaxy to learn the Jedi secrets. By the time of our last travel together, I was already in my 40s. I was ranked *godan*. I had a Ph.D. and a university professorship, and I had a wife and two daughters vying for my attention. Indeed, it cost much to have this type of relationship with my *sensei*, and despite the payment it would ultimately exact, it was well worth the cost.

This was the manner of respect in which I *chose* to treat my *sensei*. He never asked why I slept on the floor. He never told me to book a room with double beds. This was just the way it was. And whatever I lost in flesh or in the indignity of setting aside any self-righteous entitlement, I gained in secrets and insights into 16th-century *kendō*—graciously given to me by a gentleman who was still living in that 16th century.

Why would I have slept on the floor when it would have taken virtually no effort to request two beds instead of one king? Etsu Inagaki Sugimoto gives us a beautiful passage in *A Daughter of the Samurai: How a Daughter of Feudal Japan,*

Living Hundreds of Years in One Generation, Became a Modern American (1926), in which we read a young Japanese girl's recollections and perceptions of her *samurai* culture. Here, as the young girl covers her sick dog, Shiro, with her crepe *kakebuton* (blanket), her grandmother gently explains that "the boundary line between the orders of creation must be strictly maintained." More important, the grandmother explains *why* these boundaries must be maintained and why each must sleep (and behave) according to his station.

It's a book well worth reading, although I suppose it would be dismissed as utter nonsense by most of today's students.

6. Facing Death on a Weekly Basis

I could have learned so much more from Kotaka *Sensei*, especially during our long drives to his demonstrations and seminars. *Sensei* was always very open with me, much more so than I deserved. I could ask him anything, and did so. But I soon learned not to ask questions on road trips.

Sensei loved to drive. Fast. When *Sensei* was behind the wheel, driving in silence and practicing *enzan no metsuke* (eyes glazed over in "distant mountain gaze"), the mile markers on the side of the highway would whir together. It is not an exaggeration to say that this created the visual image of a solid steel fence running along the passenger side of the car.

No matter how simple or complex the question, *Sensei* would abruptly slam his foot onto the brake pedal and begin driving as if he were in a school zone. He never seemed to notice that my forehead would smack into the dashboard or that *bōgu* and *shinai* would tumble from the backseat into the front, and he would be oblivious to cars and trucks swerving around us. We were an island, awash in a sea of horns and angry drivers passing us with hand gestures that would make a sailor blush.

And then, after he had slowly and methodically answered my question, my body would be pinned in position, held fast by our acceleration back to warp speed.

Yes, I could have learned so much more from Kotaka *Sensei*. But I was too afraid to ask.

And so we drove. In silence.

7. One Doughnuts!

For the story to make sense, one must first understand that there is no plural object in the Japanese language. One understands the difference between one and many by context; consequently, it is absolutely correct for the Japanese to say one *bokken*, two *bokken*, three *bokken*, etc.

For several years, Covington, Kentucky was a normal stop on the Kotaka circuit. Rain, snow, or shine, I would wait at the top of the interstate entrance ramp in Grove City, Ohio; Kotaka *Sensei* would slow the vehicle at the intersection just enough for me to hop in, and then immediately reenter the highway with his *uchideshi* in the front seat so that we could proceed southward in the rocket mobile.

Our arrival time in Covington would be determined by how many questions I asked, but we always had time for a doughnut—because *Sensei* was never late; if he was late, you apologized for the misunderstanding and for coming too early. We would stop at the White Castle on West 3rd Street; then, we would proceed to the *Yoseikan Dōjō*, *hombu* of the United States *Chito-ryū* Federation, where Kotaka *Sensei* had been invited for Saturday lessons.

I, as senior in the *dōjō*, was expected to travel with *Sensei*. As a "junior" senior, I didn't really know what to expect, or yet understand that it was my responsibility to keep *Sensei* from killing the disrespectful Americans he would encounter during our journeys.

We walked into the White Castle; *Sensei* bellied-up to the counter and proudly ordered "one coffee, one doughnuts."

70

Whether it was a well-intended attempt at clarification or an opportunity for some high-school wise guy to jack with the old man, the youngster at the counter asked if *Sensei* wanted one doughnut or two doughnuts. "One doughnuts" came the reply. Again there was an attempt at clarification, while I was weighing whether to smack the counter boy for his insolence or to explain to my *Sensei* that it might be a better idea if I did the talking.

"ONE DOUGHNUTS! ONE DOUGHNUTS!!"

It roared through the White Castle and, I suspect, down the street. My ears are still ringing. The place went silent, and everyone turned to look at this tiny, Japanese crazy-man in Sears jeans with the eight-inch cuffs and in four-dollar Walmart sneakers. The man wanted "one doughnuts," and he wasn't going to tolerate disrespect from some teenager.

We got the "one," but I wasn't exactly sure about how to avoid what I suspected would become a weekly confrontation. Fortunately, I was to meet Bill Dometrich, head of the United States *Chito-ryū* Federation, just a few minutes after this initial confrontation.

The next week, as *Sensei* ordered his "one doughnuts," I stood behind and to his left and held up one finger, sporting an expression that made it clear that I was going to come across that counter and give a thorough beating to anyone who didn't understand that "one doughnuts" meant "ONE doughnuts."

He got his "one doughnuts," and the affair eventually became a running joke (at least among the seniors). For several years thereafter, we would arrive at the White Castle, and whoever was running the counter would announce "one coffee, one doughnuts coming right up!"

They had finally learned to speak English at the White Castle in Covington, Kentucky. And no one had to die.

8. The Near Death of an American Martial Artist

One of *Sensei's* favorite places to teach was at the *Chito -ryū dōjō* of Bill *Dometrich*, in Covington, Kentucky.

The *dōjō* was clearly a *kobudō* (traditional) *dōjō* in which Kotaka *sensei* felt at home. Okinawan weapons that were drawn from farming implements lined the wall, and it was clear from their appearance that these were not merely for show. Discipline was intense; once, when one of Bill's senior *yudansha* absentmindedly sat down in a chair while dressed in her *karate-gi*, Dometrich *Sensei* had her in the middle of the training floor doing push-ups, as punishment, in front of a full *dōjō* of *Chito-ryū* students and the invited *kendō* contingent.

Given the level of discipline in Dometrich *Sensei's dōjō*, it was a jaw-dropper when, during one of our full-day Saturday sessions, one of the *yudansha*—innocently enough, I suppose—asked how a *samurai* would respond to an attack with *nunchaku*; at the moment, this *yudansha* stepped out on the floor and whipped through a series of movements with the weapon.

Kotaka *Sensei's* facility with the English language was less than stellar (as we know from the doughnut incident), and the perceived disrespect caught him by surprise.

Typically, one holds the *tsuba* (guard of the sword) with the left thumb, securing the *katana* (sword) in the airtight *saya* (scabbard) so that, if the wearer would bend forward, the *katana* won't slip out and fall to the floor (or worse, cause the wearer to grab the blade of a 29-inch razorblade as it slides out of the scabbard). In preparation for a confrontation, one simply straightens his thumb, which breaks the airtight seal and which allows the *katana* to be quickly drawn from the scabbard without any hang-up.

In addition to the basic hold on the *tsuba*, one can also grasp the scabbard at the *koiguchi* (mouth of the *saya*) and simply "squeeze to open." This simple squeeze, which, by the compression of the hand, "pops" the *tsuba* away from the scabbard to break the seal and ready the *katana* for action, is virtually imperceptible.

At the instant this *yudansha* stepped out on the floor, I saw Kotaka *Sensei*'s hand squeeze the top of the scabbard and pop the *tsuba* one one-hundredth of an inch out of the *saya*. My guess, given that we never discussed the incident, is that Kotaka *Sensei* did not understand the language or the intent; all he saw was some unknown person coming across the floor, swinging a *nunchaku*.

Before I consciously understood the moment, I had grabbed the junior *kendō* student traveling with us; both of our backs slammed against the wall and my left arm was holding her across the chest. Several weapons tumbled from the wall-racks. Although it has been almost 40 years since the incident, I can still recall that the junior, pinned to the wall, may have even wet her *fundoshi* (a traditional Japanese undergarment).

Fortunately, and to his credit as a martial artist, Bill Dometrich either saw the squeeze or realized the impropriety. Or maybe he just heard the junior *kendō* student slamming into the wooden wall. Dometrich *Sensei* immediately jumped between this ancient Japanese fencing master and the *nunchaku*-wielding student and profusely apologized. Several times. As death hung heavy in the air.

Kotaka *Sensei* relaxed his grip on the *saya*, and the lesson continued without comment.

On that day, on a summer Saturday afternoon in Covington, Kentucky, Bill Dometrich saved the life of a young man who didn't yet understand that, to Kotaka Sukesaburo Sadayasu Sadao, the *dōjō* floor was a chessboard of life and death.

9. The Tiny Bell

I walked to lessons—for the simple reason that I was more interested in making a sword payment than a car payment. Although I could have convinced any one of my short list of successive girlfriends to drive the 9-mile distance between my apartment and Kotaka *Sensei's* home, there was something sacred about my 3-hour walk. Loaded down with a *katana, bōgu,* a *bokken,* a couple of *shinai,* and a backpack, I looked like a prehistoric Spinosaurus, with sticks of various sort protruding both vertically and horizontally.

I rather enjoyed the walk "to" practice; it would be daylight, and I'd stop at the McDonald's on Morse Road to use the restroom and fuel up on caffeine.

The walk home was somewhat less pleasant. After a four-hour beating, I would be dragging my exhausted self southward, still loaded down with a *katana, bōgu,* a *bokken,* a couple of *shinai,* and a backpack, but newly adorned with red welts and black-and-blue marks. When it was raining, it was miserable. I covered myself and my arsenal of sticks and sword by poking my head through a 55-gallon garbage bag. In late fall and winter, it was even more miserable—slugging through icy rain, slush, or snow.

A fairly large portion of my walk took me through some unsavory industrial sections of Columbus, and I often felt uncomfortable walking through the graveyards of dark warehouses and parking lots filled with tractor trailers. Alone. After midnight. In the days before cell phones. Still, I suspect that the mere sight of this prehistoric Spinosaurus, limping along, led more than one mugger to rethink the plan. And, after all, I did carry a *shinken.*

But what I feared most along my route was "the Rottweiler," always sleeping—whether in June or in mid-winter January—on a house porch on Indianola Avenue. That ****** dog would always wait until I had just passed the house and, no matter on which side of the street I'd be walking, bolt across the lawn and attempt to latch on to my leg. The first time it happened, he caught me unaware; thereafter, I'd have my *shinai* in hand. Much shouting would accompany our combat, man against dog.

Finally, Kotaka *Sensei* reached the end of his patience with my inability to figure out how to avoid the confrontation.

He took a safety pin and attached a tiny brass bell, about the size of a marble, to my backpack. He told me that he didn't want to lose me.

Off I went, southward, with my *katana*, *bōgu*, a *bokken*, a couple of *shinai*, a backpack, newly acquired red welts and black-and-blue marks, and "the bell." Each step gave off one jingle.

Just as *Sensei* had predicted, tonight was different. I saw the dog, far off down the street. The stillness seemed to amplify the low, trembling growl that usually preceded one bark and then the attack. My eyes were glued to his as he slowly turned his head to follow me as I walked past his domain and off into the distance. I watched him even after I was several blocks past his attack zone, figuring that the sneaky bastard would wait until I turned around before jumping off the porch to come running at full speed.

Within a month, that crazy dog would be walking alongside me as I passed his property, wagging his tail. Evidently, the bell had removed the element of surprise. I was no longer a threat to the treasures of old bicycles and the washing machine that littered the front yard, and the four-footed sentry of the realm became my escort. Buying an extra cheeseburger at the McDonald's, which I would toss to him when we reached the end of his domain, probably didn't hurt.

Years later, *Sensei* asked me if I still had his bell. Yes, I did. He told me that he had pinned the bell onto my backpack as a symbolic gesture, so that I wouldn't get lost and so that, if I did become lost, he could find me.

He had no recollection of my ever telling him about "the dog," and he certainly hadn't given me the bell to ward off any canine attacker. He had pinned a bell to my backpack so that I would be constantly reminded that I somehow belonged to him, and so that I would be easier to locate if I wandered (philosophically) off of the path—sort of like a shepherd coming after one of his lost sheep. I felt pretty silly about the misunderstanding, but we had a good laugh about it.

I still have the bell, hanging in our *dōjō*; it remains one of my most cherished possessions.

For other and somewhat sentimental reasons, I occasionally wear my father's dog tags on the anniversaries of his three beach landings (one of which, at Cape Gloucester, was on Christmas Day). And I give each of my new students their own set of tags. As they wear these and hear the muffled jingle of the metal plates throughout the day, I hope they're reminded of who they are, how they're expected to behave, and who they could become.

And maybe it'll protect them from dogs.

10. "You are all doing very well"

Like clockwork, we would bow out at the end of our *kendō* practice and *Sensei* would look down the row and say, with the greatest of sincerity, "This was a good practice. You are all doing very well."

Although practice was merciless and "accidents" (always intentional when inflicted by the master) were commonplace, and while not even our slightest misstep or variation from what he told us to do was overlooked, his end-of-practice praise was always the same. Word-for-word. To be honest, I don't know if it was because of his limited facility with the English language or if it was because we were all so pathetic that this was all he could muster up.

One day, I asked *Sensei* why he considered this particular night's practice—which, to me, hadn't seemed any different than any other night's practice—was a "good" practice.
"No one died."

11. Kiri-otoshi

Note: *"Ittō"* [one], *"kiri-otoshi"* [cutting down], and *"ittō saku ban tō"* [one equals ten thousand swords] are the three fundamental principles of the *Ittō-ryū*. While we often see *kiri-otoshi* ("cutting down") referred to, badly, in online discussions as a *"waza,"* (technique), *kiri-otoshi* was believed by many Japanese *samurai* to be the greatest of all combat principles; other styles—such as the *Kashima Shinto-ryū* (*hitotsu tachi*) and the *Yagyu Shinkage-ryū* (*gasshi-uchi*)—have similar strategies.

Simple as though it may appear, *kiri-otoshi* is the signature philosophical and technical aspect of the *Ittō-ryū*. It manifests itself in, according to Dave Lowry in his *Traditions: Essays on the Japanese Martial Arts and Ways* (2002), "a daring sense of timing and an absolute confidence in an ability to make a single, expertly executed technique at precisely the right moment."

That is easier said than done.

My first experience with *kiri-otoshi* was wholly unsatisfactory. Kotaka *Sensei* explained that he would cut from *jodan* directly into my skull; I was to cut from *jodan* directly into his skull. Theoretically, my blade would deflect his and I wouldn't end up on the floor with blood leaking from my nose and ears.

Like the apostle Peter, in the story of his momentary walk on the Sea of Galilee, I feared and I doubted. I had seen Kotaka *Sensei* walk on water (or at least perform the *kendō*-equivalent of such) a thousand times and yet, at that last instant when his *bokken* was travelling toward my head at perhaps 50 or 60 miles per hour, I flinched. I performed what could best be described as "cranial *tai-sabaki*" (evasive head movement), and his *bokken* struck deep into my shoulder.

We tried it once again, with the same outcome.

On the third attempt, Kotaka *Sensei* smacked me straightway on the head, knocking me to the ground. Unconscious. Later, Craig Campbell (who I suspect secretly hoped this would be his moment to become senior of the *dōjō*) told me that he and the small group of others thought that *Sensei* might have indeed killed me.

The concussion prevented me from training for several weeks, and it was a year or more before *Sensei*, once again, broached the subject of *kiri-otoshi*. To be sure, on the next attempt, my *bokken* sped through the air at an exact perpendicular angle to the floor. *Sensei's bokken* be damned, I was determined to do it his way—however illogical it sounded—or die in the process; if I flinched, I was probably going to die in any case. His *bokken* exploded to the side and my *kissaki* (point edge) stopped just touching the hairline atop his forehead.

Kotaka *Sensei* often said that "one injury is worth ten thousand explanations." This was how training was conducted in the *dōjō*. Always. It was like this even with a white belt showing up for his first practice (which explains why there were so many "first" lessons and so few "second" lessons). There was no holding back, no room for error, no opportunity to repeat something that—on the battlefield—would have spelled the difference between life and death.

Still, in hindsight to that evening, I have to ask myself: "Didn't this gentleman realize that you just can't kill a student and then simply write it off as a training accident?"

12. "Yeah, keep going"

I remember the draw with painstaking clarity. As was his practice, *Sensei* would sit in *seiza* about 20 feet in front of us, one at a time, going down the *shimoseki* (student line) from the uppermost seat to the lowest, as we demonstrated the *seiza-no-bu* (*kata*) and the *kiza-no-bu* (*kata*). Sometimes he would make a small correction; at other times, and sometimes for weeks, he would simply watch both sets of *kata*, stand up without saying a word, and then move to his right to watch the next student.

On this night, just as the *kissaki* of my *katana* left the *saya*, I twisted the *saya* just a fraction of a second too early. I didn't hear the blade slice through the wood, but I did feel the deep, stinging inch-long cut that nearly removed the thumb from my left hand.

Hot liquid covered my hand; my stomach turned to ice. To make matters worse and to add to my well-justified panic, I was wearing a white *hakama*, and we were practicing in a room that was lined with mirrors. Bright red blood was flowing down the left side of my *hakama*, the floor was slippery and then quickly became sticky, and I was watching the event in the mirror in real time—without needing to look down to see that this was bad. Very bad.

In an American *dōjō*, someone would have dialed 911 for an ambulance, or at least the wounded student would have been thrown into the backseat of the rocket mobile for a death-defying ride to the emergency room.

Kotaka *Sensei* didn't blink. He sat. Expressionless. Watching me continue through the *kata*. I hoped for the slightest acknowledgment that I had just cut my thumb off and that losing that thumb might justify—at least for tonight—foregoing the *kiza-no-bu*. I was not to be so lucky. He continued to sit. Motionless. Expressionless.

Once I completed *nuki-uchi*, the final *kata* of the *kiza-no-bu*, *Sensei* stood without saying a word and moved to the next student.

Craig Campbell helped me to bind the dangling thumb to my hand with a *tenugui*; after bowing out, he walked with me to the emergency room so a doctor could stitch my blood-crusted hand back together. Today, it's a conversation piece. I can pull my right thumb to a 90-degree angle from my pointer finger; my left thumb, still bearing the scars from my inattention to whipping a 29-inch razorblade out of a softwood tube, moves only to a fraction of that angle.

In all the remaining years we spent together, *Sensei* never mentioned the incident.
Was he a madman? By an American yardstick— yes!

Absolutely!

13. The Practical Value of "Yeah, keep going"

     After practice, when the group would go to Tommy's Pizza to recover from that particular night's beating, we'd often chide one another to move faster through the buffet line, or to finish eating, or to continue with a story from which one had been side-tracked. "Yeah, keep going." We had heard that phrase so many times—when we were winded, when we had been knocked down to the floor, when we had dropped our *shinai* because our practice partner missed the cuff of the *kote* and we weren't yet sure that the bones in our forearm hadn't been crushed by the sheer force of the blow. We heard that phrase from *Sensei* even when it made no sense to say it, so we just continued the tradition.

     I can remember hearing his voice saying "Yeah, keep going" in 1981, in Prague, when I was frantically dodging through the back alleys to make my way to the Marine garrison at the U.S. Embassy. As an American citizen who had carried letters from dissidents abroad into a Communist state, and as a Christian who entered the country with Bibles, I was the target of a sting operation drawn up by the Czech secret police. If it weren't for a Marine guard at the Embassy grabbing me by the jacket and dragging me into the compound, onto "American" soil, I might have spent the next several years in a Czech prison.

     I can remember hearing his voice in 1989, in Guatemala. I had the simple task of delivering an envelope to the home of one of the presidential candidates, who happened to be living in a heavily fortified and armed mansion in Antigua. Easy. Deliver the envelope, hopefully have dinner with super-rich folk, go home. After dinner, I, and the two Guatemalans who had been charged with looking after me, stopped at a local street carnival. While I was calling attention to myself (i.e., showing off), demonstrating the not-so-average marksmanship that had been passed down from my father, someone brushed aside my two bodyguards and stabbed me in the stomach with an ice pick. Anti-American hostility was at its peak; bleeding from the pick wound, three of us crashed through vendors and across tables—creating havoc and probably injuring more than a few innocents—as we were chased by a group of angry, machete-wielding teenagers. Before we could get to a hospital, I spent the night sleeping—and bleeding—in the jungle.

I can remember hearing his voice in 1999, in Columbus, Mississippi. I was out for an early-morning jog; I was run over by a drunk driver. I can remember hearing—in the emergency room—that I wasn't ever again going to be able to walk. My first attempt at disproving this initial assessment resulted in hauling my miserable carcass out of the hospital bed and promptly falling face-first onto the floor. But I continued to be haunted by "Yeah, keep going"—from the first shuffle in a body cast while hunched over a walker to the first time I turtled around the walking track at Propst Park. I'm still a hopeless cripple, but I can walk . . . thanks to some crazy Japanese fellow who taught me what can be accomplished through nothing more than self-discipline.

What was the point of being expected to focus on the task at hand (no pun intended) after cutting off my thumb with a long razorblade? What was the point of "Yeah, keep going"? It wasn't until years later that I fully grasped the significance.

14. Cutting Apples

My favorite part of training was our solitary practice, cutting leaves in the autumn. *Sensei* and I would go to Blendon Woods (a 653-acre state park in Columbus, Ohio) just after dawn, find a place that was far from the eyes of nosy civilians, and uncase our *katana*. He would wrap the *tsuka* (handle) of his *katana* in gauze, just as his ancestors would have done prior to battle—to soak up the blood and to allow for a more secure grip. Then, in the crisp autumn air, we would, with a single motion, draw-cut-and-return the *katana* to the *saya*.

It didn't take long for me to understand that there was a great distance between "hitting" a leaf and "cutting" a leaf. On a calm morning, when a leaf might fall from the tree and float gently to the earth, swaying slightly in the wind, two or three might die by my sword; in a thunderstorm, when visibility was reduced to zero and when leaves were being ripped from the branches by a howling wind, *Sensei*—with a self-satisfied smile on his lips—would be surrounded by a ring of red and yellow half-leaves, each neatly sliced in two.

This is the memory of Kotaka *Sensei* I most cherish. He was reliving the scene directly out of *Seven Samurai*, where Kyuzo, the master swordsman, goes off for solitary training in the rain . . . and I was privileged to watch.

In the *dōjō*, when we would catch a glimpse of him out of the corner of our eye (instead of being focused on our own practice), he would be standing in front of the mirror, practicing *kamae*. That's correct, his *kamae* . . . his posture, how he would present himself to an adversary. "We" were slicing and dicing our way through an imaginary battlefield with *katate-waza* (one-handed techniques) and the *tsubame gaeshi* (swallowtail cut) and the flying mongoose of Chicago; after a half-century, *Sensei* was still working to perfect "standing."

I never mastered "leaf-cutting," but *Sensei* would often soothe my disappointment and bruised ego with an armful of apples. He would hike up his *hakama* into a makeshift basket, collect two or three dozen apples, and then toss them at me—underhanded, like in girls' softball, but in slow motion. It was a baby step on the road to becoming a competent swordsman, but I did indeed love cutting apples with my *sensei*.

He was always very kind to me in this way.

15. The 40-Year Bruise

Anyone who is reading this understands about *kime* (focus) and that damage isn't necessarily done to the "surface" of the target.

Kotaka *Sensei* hit me once by accident. I have no doubt that I, in my ignorance, somehow positioned my left thigh in a place and manner that would be incomprehensible to anyone even remotely familiar with *kendō*. I can't imagine how I could have made my left thigh a target. But he hit me with his *shinai*. Kotaka *Sensei* hit me, by accident, with a flimsy bamboo *shinai*, in the mid-1970s. Several times a year that wound still aches, even after four decades. There is no longer any visible mark where his *shinai* wrapped across my thigh, but, on these occasions, I can run my finger around a seven-inch swath of a wound that's never going to heal.

Think about that if you're playing "sport" *kendō* and impressed with your ability to score with "tap-points." Some of those old-school dinosaurs could kill you with nothing more than a cardboard tube of Christmas wrap. Kotaka *Sensei* was one of those dinosaurs.

16. The Death of Courtesy

I asked him, once, what he considered to be the most important lesson of the martial arts.

"To be polite."

He lamented the deterioration of discourse on the martial-art websites and the rise of a generation of ill-mannered "punks" (his word), hiding behind ridiculous Internet pseudonyms while posting disrespectful slander against even the most senior of instructors—instructors who were stomping ass since dinosaurs roamed the earth.

He never understood how such disrespect would be levied against any instructor who didn't fall within the ant-sized world of the self-appointed Internet archangels (again, his word) and who, in another time, he would have simply killed for their loudmouthed insolence.

And yet he had a wonderful sense of humor. He caught me totally off-guard when he summarized his observation of "spiritual development," as it was being taught in American karate studios: "Don't kick Billy in the balls."

To be honest, I don't think he liked teaching Americans.

Come to think of it, I'm an American, and I'm not sure that I like teaching Americans.

17. The Circus

Sensei had four children. Yuji was the youngest, and he occasionally practiced with our group. It was a comedy show. Big burly *kendō-ka* had to carefully watch that we didn't trample the 5-year-old, barely visible to us when we were wearing the *men*.

But we loved having him around. He would regularly ask his father annoying questions such as "Dad, would your sword cut rope?" Forty years later, Larry Wilcoxen and I are still using this question in place of "Does a duck like water?" It's a gem of Kotaka-wit that has even crept into my own teaching as an idiom of good-natured sarcasm.

In any case, Yuji was one of "us."

At one point, we asked Mr. and Mrs. Kotaka if we could take Yuji to the circus that had come to town. Although we were *gaijin* (non-Japanese, ill-mannered, foreign devils), they agreed.

What a sight we must have made! Little Yuji and three *kendō-ka* of the *Sakurai-ha Kogen Ittō-ryū*. We had that little kid surrounded as if we were the Secret Service protecting the President. If you messed with this kid's cotton candy, we would have broken every bone in your body. If you even looked at this kid, there would be hell to pay.

I hope Yuji doesn't remember it in quite this way, and just remembers it as the time "the guys" took him to the circus. I don't know how his old man put up with us.

18. The Christian *Samurai*

What did I know? Hollywood had taught me that all Japanese martial artists were mystic Zen Buddhists; Kotaka *Sensei* was, therefore, by logic, a mystic Zen Buddhist.

When I—as a former seminary student and with a background in Medieval-Renaissance history and Bible apologetics—broached the subject of how Japanese ethics and behavior could be reconciled with Christian tenants, I was immediately set straight about my Hollywood perceptions of the *samurai*. And I heard an earful about the bashing of Japanese martial arts by uninformed Christian zealots in America.

Without batting an eyelid, he rattled off a long list (abbreviated here) of Christian *samurai*:

- Zaisho Shichiemon (dates unknown), martyred, beatified by the Catholic Church in 2008;
- Kuroda Yoshitaka (1546-1604), chief strategist and adviser to Toyotomi Hideyoshi;
- Ukon Takayama (1552-1615), currently under consideration for sainthood in the Catholic Church;
- Masuda Jinbei (dates unknown), martyred, later the protagonist in the 2007 Christian movie "Good Soil";
- Amakusa Shirō (1621-1638), son of Masuda Jinbei and teenaged leader of the Catholic-Shimabara Rebellion;
- Tsukue Gen'noshin Humitaka ("Ryunosuke Tsukue," dates unknown), a *samurai* within Kotaka *Sensei*'s own lineage who converted to Christianity after becoming blind and who spent the rest of his life teaching swordsmanship and the Gospel to children—in what may have been the first Christian *kendō dojo*;
- Sasamori Junzō (1886-1976), Christian minister and 16th headmaster of the *Ono-ha Ittō-ryū*, author of the seminal work on *kendō*, *This is Kendō: The Art of Japanese Fencing* (1964); and
- Sasamori Takemi (son of Sasamori Junzō, 1933-), Christian minister and 17th headmaster of the *Ono-ha Ittō-ryū*.

To throw additional salt into my display of ignorance, *Sensei* then proceeded to quiz "me"—the university-trained hotshot Bible apologist—about how I could not see the great parallels between Japanese ethics, Japanese *kōans*, and the King James Version.

Kotaka *Sensei* was a man of complex spirituality with feet firmly planted in two very different worlds. We shared many private moments about God and curses, about honor and duty, and about logic and faith.

While those conversations were personal and private,

85

the upshot was to be The All-Texas Christian Women's *Kendō* Federation, a martial-art ministry *by* women and *for* women. The purpose of this organization, which has now spread across Texas and up into the Panhandle, is twofold: to preserve the classical warrior traditions of the Japanese *onna-bugeisha* (female warriors of the *samurai* class) within re-creations of the traditional fencing school of 16th-century Japan and to use the small wooden world of the *dōjō* as the seedbed for intimate Christian fellowship, growth in faith and understanding, and joyful service.

19. Two Sheets of Notebook Paper

When Kotaka *Sensei* awarded me the *renshi menkyo* in 1992 and bade me to carry on the legacy of the *Sakurai-ha Kogen Ittō-ryū*, he called me to sit with him in his living room. It was the conveying of the Biblical birthright, the parental blessing, and the award of the paper credential to back up what I already had, with or without a sheet of parchment.

As always, Kotaka *Sensei* was the embodiment of *shibui* (simple elegance) with comic absurdity.

As I unfolded the first piece of paper, which was pre-sented to me with great ceremony, I saw that he had neatly typed "Congatulation on receiving *renshi menkyo.*" This was it. My formal teaching license in the *Sakurai-ha Kogen Ittō-ryū* consists of five words on a sheet of notebook paper. He was beside himself with laughter when he pointed out, repeatedly, that he had purchased a new ribbon for his typewriter for just this occasion.

On the second sheet of paper is what I've come to be-lieve is the essence of how he perceived the *Sakurai-ha Kogen Ittō-ryū*. It explained what I was supposed to do in my own *dōjō*. It would become the *bunkai* of the All-Texas Christian Women's *Kendō* Federation.

Note: The term *bunkai* is usually translated as "disassembly" or "deconstruction" or "analysis." The term is most-often applied to the explanation of hidden meanings within a prearranged sequence of movements within a *kata*. On the surface, the movements are practiced as a dance to teach balance, rhythm, timing, etc.; at a deeper level, the *kata* serves as a catalog of obvious—as well as hidden—techniques which, if practiced apart from the sequence, might easily be forgotten.

The term *bunkai*, however, can also convey a much deeper meaning. It is the explanation of why one particular hand- or foot-strike or *kata* or weapon is included in the curriculum while another is left aside. Thus, the *bunkai* is not only the foundation of everything that is taught in the *dōjō*, but it forms the philosophical basis of the *ryū-ha*. Without a well-formulated *bunkai*, the curriculum of a *dōjō* would be little more than a collection of unrelated techniques which, while perhaps lethal in and of themselves, do not prepare a particular type of student for a particular type of combat.

I wept, and later I would be glad that our relationship could end with this as its final memory.

Indeed, I became so caught up with family, school, and distance that this was the last time that I saw him, and I miss him dearly.

The Japanese say that a man dies twice: first, when he leaves the body; then again when his memory is forgotten.

As long as we continue to practice the *Sakurai-ha Kogen Ittō-ryū*, Kotaka Sukesaburo Minamotono Sadayasu Sadao, my *sensei*, remains alive.

20. The Last Teaching of Kotaka Sadao

Bunkai of the All-Texas Christian Women's *Kendō* Federation:

We must accept that discourtesy, cruelty, and apathy mark the nature of humankind and that the resulting violence—or the threat of violence—has resolved every major conflict in the history of the world.

There is no such thing as a good war or a glorious war

or a "just" war. There is only "war," and it is always miserable. The better we attend to our training and to our responsibilities, the less the chance we will be forced to intervene. In preparation for that moment, everything must be perfect . . . or not at all.

In preparation for that moment, it is the forging of (self) discipline—the will to do what must be done—that must be the primary goal in training for combat.

It is our station to remain unseen in all things and, if seen, then in all things polite. Discernment and courtesy can be the sharpest of weapons in destroying the enemy's will to fight.

All conflicts are won by the perception of the battle-changing event.

The threat of our actions cannot be a credible deterrent if our enemy knows that our actions will be measured "in kind" or administered under civilized "rules of engagement." Deterrence comes not from our ability to overwhelm the enemy, but from a perceived willingness that we will horribly and mercilessly punish that enemy.

We must expect that the fight, or the necessity to intervene, will come by surprise and to our least advantage.

Training for the inevitable combat must be practical. Fighting on hardwood must be no different than fighting in the *ryokan* (Japanese inn) or in a snowstorm. Night-fighting must be practiced, as well.

The fight will rarely be one against one, but one against many. The chief danger is being caught by many hands and forced down to the floor; restraints, choke-holds, and ground fighting must therefore be avoided.

There is a simple logic to warfare: we win by punishing the enemy more than the enemy has punished us. Controlled violence may destroy the enemy's will to fight, may give us opportunity to assess the situation for further action, and may allow us to strategically delay or reposition for a larger battle. If, however, the enemy is killing many or wounding much, guilt or innocence can no longer be a factor, and we must be prepared to get on with it.

Once it becomes necessary to fight, we must close with the enemy at the earliest possible moment. We must strike simply and quickly and with total commitment. We must never prance around like a dandy and never make two cuts when one will suffice; these affectations distract our attention from the only matter that is relevant, which is to deal with each attacker one time only and to a conclusive end.

Combat is not a game to be lightly entered. We must accept that, once engaged, the element of chance is ever-present, and that there is but a one-in-three chance to survive.

Kotaka Sadao demonstrating *Iaido* at the Covington, KY *karate dojo* of *Hanshi* William Dometrich.

Photo courtesy of Hisako Kotaka.

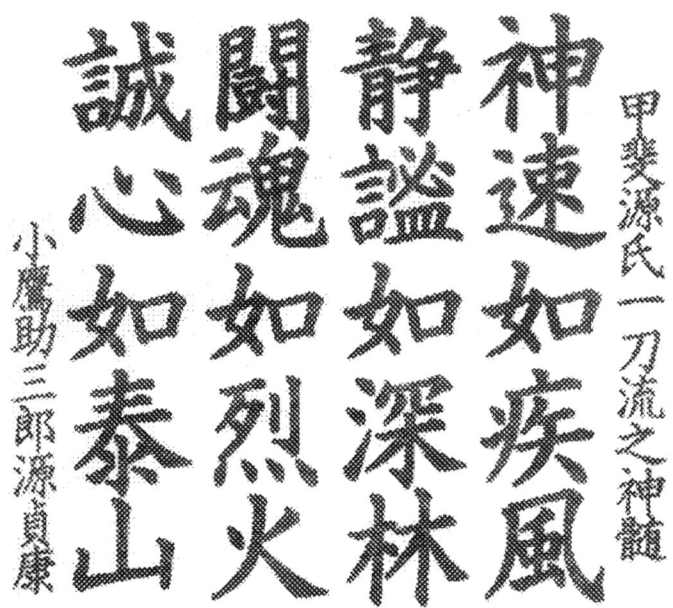

誠　闘　静　神　甲
心　魂　謐　速　斐
如　如　如　如　源
泰　烈　深　疾　氏
山　火　林　風　一
　　　　　　　　刀
小　　　　　　流
鷹　　　　　　之
助　　　　　　神
三　　　　　　髄
郎
源
貞
康

"The Spirit of the Kai-genji (Kogen) Itto-ryu"

Action as swift as a divine gale.
Poise for opening as tranquil as a deep forest.
Fighting spirit as fierce as a blazing fire.
Determination as immobile as Taisan Mountain.

Kotaka Sukesaburo Minamotono Sadayasu

Kotaka Sadao's Style and Kogen Itto-ryu

Overleaf: Kotaka *Sensei* (right) practicing *iaijutsu* with a senior student. Photo from the now defunct website of the United States Classical Kendo Federation.

Following is a description of the history and style Kotaka Sadao claimed to represent and some of the questions and controversy those claims aroused. The author is not in a position to assess the validity of Kotaka *Sensei*'s version of history, though it does raise some difficult questions, which will be discussed in the next chapter. Moreover, as Kotaka *Sensei* aged and attempted to establish his United States Classical Kendo Federation, his comments and claims sometimes became more strident and more difficult to understand. Part of the reason for this appears to have been annoyance at being questioned by people who had never met him, including some with limited experience in *kenjutsu*, Japanese culture, history, and language. Part may have been due to the effects of a worsening cognitive condition from the late 1990s until his death.

Questions of history and historical connection to the still extant Henmi family *Kogen Itto-ryu* notwithstanding, Kotaka Sadao was an outstanding *kenkaku* (swordsman), as attested to by everyone who met him sword-to-sword. The previous chapter reproduced a number of testimonies to his ability by highly accomplished *kenshi* (swordsmen) who had the opportunity to train or cross swords with him.

This chapter will begin with a description of the precursors, history and nature of "*Itto-ryu*," followed by a description and history of the "*Kogen Itto-ryu*" as currently taught in Japan. It will then discuss Kotaka *Sensei*'s account of the style he came to call "*Sakurai-ha Kogen Ittoryu*" or "*Sakurai-ha Kai Genji Itto-ryu*."*

The next chapter will discuss the times and nature of the *Shinsengumi* from which Kotaka *Sensei* claimed his style derived. These links, I believe, will shed light on why there is such a radical difference between the "*Kogen Itto-ryu*" he taught and the "*Kogen Itto-ryu*" still taught by the Henmi family in Japan.

---

* Sometimes *Sensei* would spell his style "*Kohgen Itto-ryu*." This is simply a stylistic difference; neither the Japanese characters (*kanji*) nor the meaning is different.

Precursors to Itto-ryu

Swordsmanship in Japan goes back to the pre-historic era, when stone swords were used; archaeologists have actually found the skeleton of a man from 200-250 BC with what is believed to be a stone sword point embedded in one of his thoracic vertebrae.[1] Moreover, the mythology upon which the very Japanese society, culture, religion, and political system were founded began with the god Izanagi and his sister-wife, goddess Izanami, creating the Japanese islands by dripping water from a spear.[2]

Divine origins of the sword. They dispatched two warrior-gods—Takemi-kazuchi and Futsunushi-no-Mikoto—to rule Japan. Futsunushi landed at the site later sanctified as the Katori shrine and became the *kami* (spirit) of swords and lightning. It is from this shrine that one of the major lineages of Japanese *Kenjutsu* (swordsmanship)—the *Katori-ryu*—traces its ancestry.[3] Takemi-kazuchi is said to have landed not far away, at the current site of the Kashima shrine, becoming the *kami* of thunder and swords, and taking place in the first *sumo* contest.

The legendary first emperor of Japan, Jimmu Tenno (神武天皇, allegedly ascended to the throne in 660 BC) had bestowed upon him the sword named *Futsu-no-mitama-no-tsurugi,* which is said to be stored in the Kashima shrine. His descendant, Yamato-no Takeru (日本武尊, allegedly c.72-133 AD), became famous for wielding his sword *Kusanagi* (Grass-cutter) while attempting to subdue eastern Japan to the rule of the imperial dynasty.[4]

Proliferation of schools. Thus Japan can truly be said to have been born to the sword. Swordsmanship evolved over hundreds of years, alongside the technologies imported from China and Korea and the innovations of Japan's sword makers and users. While the sword did not become the principal weapon of the warrior until the 16th and 17th centuries, it was always an object of intense study and veneration. During the many years of warfare in the Japanese middle ages, sword masters established schools in which to teach the warriors of each lord, but few of these traditions—*kaden*, or "house traditions"—have survived intact.[5] However, "Specialized swordsmanship skills as a separate system apparently did not develop extensively until the late Muromachi (1336-1573) era, most [developed] significantly after the introduction of firearms."[6]

By the beginning of the Edo Era (the Tokugawa shogunate, 1600), swordsmanship styles had proliferated profligately: the oldest catalogue of such schools—the *Bugei Shoden* (around 1600)—listed approximately 1,700 *ryu* (styles) and *ryu-ha* (derivative styles or branches). Many of these died out, but toward the end of the Edo era in the 1860s, another catalogue listed 52 separate schools/styles of *kyudo* (archery), 718 styles of *Kenjutsu* (swordsmanship), 148 styles of *sojutsu* (spearmanship), 92 styles of *naginata-jutsu* (for fighting with the halberd), and 178 schools of *jujutsu* (unarmed self-defense.)[7]

The "Three Great Schools." Ultimately, experts have narrowed down the number of ancestral, source, or "Ur-schools" to a much smaller number. Many experts consider there to have been "Three Great Schools" ("*San Dai Ryu*") or "Three Great Source Schools" ("*San Dai Gen Ryu*"), all dating to the 1300s or 1400s. Not all experts, however, agree on which three should be accorded this honor.[8] In general, however, there is largely agreement that:

1. The **Nen-ryu** is probably the oldest, established in the late 1300s. (It will be discussed below as the ancestor of the *Itto-ryu* styles.)
2. The next oldest is the **Shinto-ryu** of Iizasa Choisai (1387?-1488), from which are descended the "*Kanto Shichi-ryu*" (The Seven Schools of the Kanto, or eastern Japan plain) also called the "*Kashima Shichi-ryu*" (The Seven Schools of the Kashima Shrine lineage.) These include the *Tenshin Shoden Katori Shinto-ryu, Kashima Shin-ryu, Kashima Shinto-ryu, Kashima Shinden Jiki Shinkage-ryu, Arima Shinto-ryu, Ichiu-ryu* (also known as the *Ichiu Hau-ryu* or *Ippa-ryu*), *Shinto Munen-ryu, Shinto Muso-ryu, Ten-ryu, Tenshinsho*

95

Jigen-ryu, Jigen-ryu, and the *Tennen Rishin-ryu* (to which we shall return when we discuss the possible role of the Shinsengumi in the development of Kotaka Sadao's *"Sakurai-ha Kogen Itto-ryu).*

3. The most recent is the **Kage-ryu** ("Shadow style") of Aisu Ikosai Hisatada (1452?-1538?). From the *Kage-ryu* emerged the *Shinkage-ryu, Hikita Kage-ryu, Shinkage-Okuyama-ryu, Yagyu Shinkage-ryu, Taisha-ryu, Shin Shinkage-ryu, Jikishinkage-ryu, Shinnuki-ryu,* and *Mujushinken-ryu.*

Nen-ryu,* ancestor of *Itto-ryu. *Nen-ryu Kenjutsu* was founded around the 1370s or 1380s by a monk of the Rinzai school of Zen whose original name was Soma Shiro Yoshimoto (相馬 四 郎 義元), who was born about 1351.[9] According to the history/legends surrounding the style, he was the fourth son of a *samurai* in the service of the major warlord Nitta Yoshisada. (The Nitta, by the way, are also descendants of Seiwa, and thus a sub-clan of the Seiwa Genji.) The father, Tadashige, was an expert archer in Yoshisada's army, but was assassinated when Yoshimoto was only five years old.

Yoshimoto's wet nurse took the child and fled from Oshu, in northern Japan, to Musashi province, now Saitama and Tokyo prefectures. At the age of seven, he was left in the care of a wandering priest named Yugyu who spent much of his time in present-day Kanagawa prefecture, near Kamakura. He joined the Jufuku-ji, the oldest Zen temple in Kanagawa, and the third most prestigious of the so-called "Five Mountains of Zen," or the five great Zen monasteries of the time. He entered the priesthood, receiving the name of "Nen Ami " (念阿弥).

Nen Ami, despite his religious vocation, however, always harbored the intent to avenge his father's murder. At the age of 10, he relocated to Mount Kurama near Kyoto, where he was taken in by the monks. There, he studied martial arts and esoteric Buddhist practices under "Ijin"* and others. At the age of 16, Nen Ami was introduced to the secret principles of

---

* According to Bekink (page 69), "Ijin" means "Outsider." He speculated Ijin may have been a Chinese. This is possible, but he may have been (continued)

kenjutsu by his mentors. At the age of 18, Nen Ami left the priesthood, went back to Oshu, and avenged his father. That filial duty accomplished, he rejoined the religious community, adding the name "Jion" (慈恩) to his Buddhist appellation.* He then began to travel all over Japan teaching and engaging in *musha shugyo* (hard training and challenge matches).

As historian Serge Mol recounts, "Over the course of his travels, he appears to have taught a number of students at various locations. Several of them founded their own schools. The names of fourteen students, which are considered his top students have been preserved. They are known as '*Jion Juyontetsu*" meaning "Jion's Fourteen Brilliant Disciples." Among them supposedly were:

- Chujo Hyogo-no-kami (or Hyogonosuke) Naga-hide, who would found the influential *Chujo-ryu*;
- Nikaido Umanosuke who created *Nikaido-ryu*;
- Tsutsumi Yamashiro-no-kami Hozan, founder of *Tsutsumi Hozan-ryu*;
- Higuchi Taro Kaneshige, founder of *Kaneshige Nen-ryu*; and
- Akamatsu Sanshuso, creator of *Nen Shuso-ryu*. Akamatsu was said to have been Jion's brother.

Each of these styles spawned additional styles, the most famous of which today is the *Maniwa Nen-ryu*.[10]

Chujo-ryu. It was from the *Chujo-ryu (中条流)*, however, that *Itto-ryu* claims its lineage.[11] One of Nan Ami Jion's most promising students reputedly was Chujo Hyogo-no-suke

---

a *Yamabushi*, a Japanese mountain ascetic and follower of *Shugendo*, an esoteric sect of Buddhism the practices of which allegedly give its followers miraculous powers. The *Yamabushi* are the subjects of numerous legends and stories in Japan. A few such *Yamabushi* still live in these mountains. Mount Kurama is also the origin of the now-popular healing art of *Reiki*. Mount Kurama was also the location at which Minamoto Yoshitsune met and studied with the King of the *Tengu*, Sojobo. In short, it is a storied and holy place in Japanese culture.

* Some *karate* experts attribute the *kata Jion* to Nen Ami Jion, almost certainly mistakenly.

Nagahide (中条長秀, died about 1384). The Chujo family had a tradition of sword and spear techniques which Chujo Naga-hide learned, but according to legend he also studied the *Nen-ryu* style of swordsmanship and the art of the spear from Nen Ami Jion. Although doubts remain about whether Chujo was actually Nen Ami's student, "there can be little doubt that the school effectively belongs to the Nen Ryu lineage, as Chujo Ryu's second head, Kai Bizen no Kami Hirokage, was also one of Jion's Fourteen Brilliant Students. It was under Kai Bizen no Kami that the school was spread in Echizen" province in west-ern Japan on the East China Sea.[12]

As historian Serge Mol relates:

> Not surprisingly, there are many schools that belong to the Chujo Ryu sphere of influence, including the Toda Ryu, the Awaga Ryu, the Togun Ryu, the Shinkyoku Ryu (also called Hasegawa Ryu), the Chujo Yamazaki Ryu, and the Kanemaki Ryu. From Kanemaki Ryu, the famous Itto Ryu was born.[13]

Descendant Styles From *Chujo-ryu*

```
                    Chujo Ryu
                        |
                    Toda Ryu
                        |
  +----------------+----+--------------+------------------+
  |                |                   |                  |
Kanemaki Ryu    Ippo Ryu           Togun Ryu        Shinkyoku Ryu
  |                |              +----+-----+
Itto Ryu       Ichimu Ryu      Shin Ryu   Ittetsu Ryu
  |                |              |
+-----+------+     +--+         Okumura
Onoha       Mitoha             Togun Ryu
Itto Ryu    Itto Ryu
  |             |
Hokushin    Itto Shoden
Itto Ryu    Muryoku Ryu


Buko Ryu
```

Source: http://wiki.samurai-archives.com/index.php?title=File:Chujo2.jpg.

Itto-ryu

Although *Itto-ryu* is not the oldest style of *kenjutsu*, it is without doubt the most influential. Modern *kendo* is based almost entirely on the techniques and principles of *Itto-ryu*, as is much of modern *iaido*. "The men instrumental in creating the technical curriculum of *kendo* (modern Japanese fencing, or swordsmanship with mock weapons made of bamboo) were greatly influenced by *Itto-ryu* theory and technique. Several of the men charged with creating the *Dai Nippon Teikoku Kendo Kata*, forerunner of today's *Nihon Kendo Kata*, were exponents of *Hokushin Itto-ryu* and they conferred with exponents of other branches of the *Itto-ryu* in order to create the forms that became the technical standard for modern *kendo*." [14]

Like other early styles, it eventually spawned a large number of "*ryu-ha*." "*Itto-ryu* has preserved a greater number of its derivative styles than any other school of *kenjutsu* and is today one of the most viable 'families' of classical Japanese swordsmanship. There are six lines of *Itto-ryu* still being practiced today, with a sufficient number of exponents and level of skill to ensure that their art will be passed on intact to future generations: *Ono-ha Itto-ryu, Mizoguchi-ha Itto-ryu, Nakanishi-ha Itto-ryu, Kogen Itto-ryu, Hokushin Itto-ryu,* and *Itto Shoden Muto-ryu*." [15]

Itto-ryu produced such famous 20th century masters as Sasamori Junzo (笹森順造, 1886-1976, 16th headmaster of the *Ono-ha Itto-ryu* and author of *This is Kendo: The Art of Japanese Fencing*), Takeda Sokaku (武田 惣角, 1859–1943, founder of *Daito-ryu Jujutsu* and teacher of Ueshiba Morihei, 植芝 盛平, founder of *Aikido),* Henmi Chifuji (9th headmaster of *Kogen Itto-ryu*), Takano Sasaburo (高野佐三郎, 1862-1950, one of the stalwarts of the pre-War *kenjutsu* world and student of the famous Yamaoka Tesshu, (山岡 鉄舟, 1836-1888), and Mochida Moriji (持田 盛二, 1885-1974), who became one of *kendo*'s earliest *Hanshi Judan*).

Great Itto-ryu Kenshi

Yamaoka Tesshu

Takeda Sokaku

Sasamori Junzo *Hanshi*

Takano Sasaburo
Hanshi

Mochida Moriji *Hanshi*

Members of the Committee to Create a *Kendo-no Kata*, 1911

Back row (left to right): Tsuji Shinpei (*Shingyoto-ryu*), Naito Takaharu (*Hokushin Itto-ryu)* and Takano Sasaburo (*Hokushin Itto-ryu*).
Sitting (left to right): Monna Tadashi (*Hokushin Itto-ryu*), and Negishi Shingoro (*Shindo Munen-ryu*).

The Founder of *Itto-ryu.*

The story of the founder of *Itto-ryu*, like most "history" from the period is a combination of truth, mythology, and fiction.[16] The following is an effort to make sense of the various stories and accounts of his origins, training, life, and death.

A rough start. In about the year 1550—or maybe it was 1560—a boy was born on the island of Oshima, a small volcanic outcropping in the Pacific about 60 miles southeast of Edo off the Izu peninsula. This "remote island...was long known as the final destination for political and religious exiles banished from the homeland." Its "sense of otherness and isolation, combined with exotic, almost alien volcanic terrain, also once attracted large numbers of visitors looking for a final destination of a different sort—young adults who made the long journey to cast themselves from its cliffs in suicide pacts."[17]

The island historically was so remote and forbidding that its most famous exile, En no Gyoja (or En no Ozunu), an eighth-century shaman, is thought to have been the founder of the mountain-worshipping religion of Shugendo (修験道), the religion followed by many of the mysterious *Yamabushi* (山伏), mountain ascetics famous throughout Japan both historically and today. En no Gyoja's rising fame and growing group of followers began frightening the emperor's advisors, who "trumped up conspiracy charges and dumped the hapless holy man on the remote island." There he spent three years meditating in a cave and "using his mastery of a magical mantra called the 'Peacock King' to literally walk across the waters on pilgrimages to Mount Fuji, hundreds of kilometers away on the mainland."[18]

Our protagonist's story was not nearly so magical or romantic. Maehara Yagoro likely was born to a low-level *samurai* or *ronin* who had been banished to the island for some unknown transgression. More than likely, his father taught him some rudiments of *kenjutsu* and possibly other martial arts, but Yagoro was rebellious, adventurous, and ambitions, a dangerous triple-threat combination.

At about the age of 13 or 14, he decided to escape his imprisonment. Whether his father had died, or he simply decided to strike out on his own is unknown, but Yagoro left the hard way. He is said to have swam, floated, and drifted holding onto a piece of wood across the Sagami Sea about 18 miles. He supposedly washed up at a village on the Izu peninsula half drowned and thoroughly bedraggled.

"Adopted." The villagers took Yagoro in, and he found a place sleeping underneath the Mishima Shrine in Ito village. There, the local priest, Yada Oribe, took young Yagoro under his wing. Yagoro already fancied himself something of a swordsman, but he apparently trained under the priest for some time, improving his skill. The shrine, though small and relatively isolated, housed a number of swords that, as was the custom, had been donated by patrons to commemorate various important events or seek favors from the *kami* (spirits or gods).

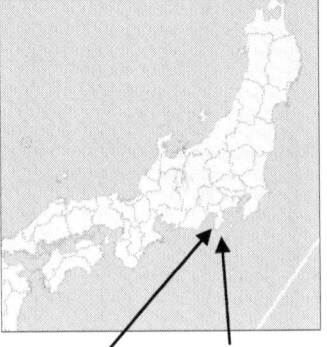

Izu Peninsula   Oshima island

One night, a gang of about six robbers who had been terrorizing the area, broke into the shrine, apparently to steal the swords and whatever other valuables they could find. Yagoro, according to legend, pounced on them—most likely surprising them by emerging from underneath the elevated building where he lived—and defeated them all. In gratitude, the villagers agreed to finance his trip to Edo to find a *kenjutsu* tutor to help him reach a higher level of skill. The priest gave Yagoro one of the shrine's swords, one made by the famous swordsmith, Ichimonji, from Fukuoka, so he could appear in the capital in a respectable style.

Off to the big city. So, Yagoro set off for the capital, intent on finding a sword master to teach him. He was full of confidence and brio, apparently having already defeated one man in a duel in Ito village in addition to taking on the bandits. Some accounts allege Yagoro studied by himself in the moun-

103

Yagoro's sword

Yagoro's sword would later become famous and would be passed down to generations of his successors. Many swords had names; his was called *"Kamewari-to"* or the "Jar-cutting Sword." Therein lies a tale—or rather several. According to one story, while fighting the bandits, the sword had fallen from its display stand and, in falling, had cut through a large earthen jar. Needless to say, this is highly unlikely, not because a sword was unable to cleave such a jar, but because the sword never would have been displayed with its blade open to the elements and in such a way that it could fall to the ground. Another account says that when Yagoro struck down one of the bandits, he cut through not only the person's body, but the large storage jar in front of which he was standing. Most probably, however, the sword likely was tested for its cutting ability not on a condemned criminal or a corpse or an unsuspecting peasant bystander, but by cutting completely through a man-sized earthen-war storage jar. Whatever the truth, the sword was ever after called "Jar-cutter" and was handed down as such.

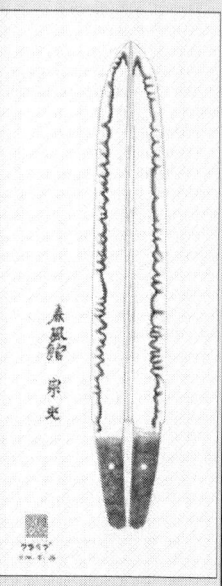

Alleged drawing of Ittosai's sword.

tains on the way to Edo; another version has him stopping off at the Tsurugaoka Hachiman shrine, a nationally-famous shrine dedicated to Minamoto Yoshiie, the posthumously-named "God of War," *Hachiman taro*. He supposedly committed himself to spending seven days and nights sleeping on the ground, practicing *kenjutsu* until exhausted. On the seventh night, he was practicing when some sixth sense alerted him to danger. He quickly spun around, drew his sword, and struck—hitting and killing an unknown swordsman who was sneaking up behind him to attack in the pitch-black darkness.[19]

Whatever adventures he may have encountered on the way, Yagoro soon arrived in Edo seeking entrance to the *Chujo -ryu dojo*, one of the most highly respected schools for teaching swordsmanship.

In any event, Yagoro seems to have wound up being accepted as a pupil by Kanemaki Jisai (鐘巻 自斎, c. 1536-1615) , one of the most famous swordsmen in Edo, a master of *Chujo-ryu*, and possibly a teacher of Sasaki Kojiro (佐々木 小次郎, c. 1585-1612), who would later supposedly fall to the *bokken* of Miyamoto Musashi in the famous duel at Ganryu Island. Jisai's teacher was Toda Seigen (富田 勢源, 1519?-1590?), a master of *Chujo-ryu* and creator of his own style, *Toda-ryu*.[20]

Yagoro quickly became one of Toda Seigen's most promising and advanced students. One day, Yagoro approached his master, shocking him by announcing that he had discovered and completely absorbed the *myogi* or deep mysteries of *kenjutsu*. Taken aback, Seigen chastised him by saying, "You have only been studying here less than five years, yet you come and tell me you have understood the secrets of sword fighting?! How arrogant!"

Undaunted, Yagoro offered to show Seigen, saying "the deeper mysteries I discovered by myself, they were not taught by a teacher, and it is not a matter of how long or short the study period it, enlightenment is a matter of an instant."[21] Jisai, in effect, told young Yagoro, "OK, young whipper-snapper, let's see your secrets."

Perhaps Jisai should not have been so surprised: Yagoro was a rather crude, abrupt, and unpleasant fellow, as we shall see later. This hardly seems so astounding given the hard road he had traveled and his largely self-made path in life. In any event, according to one account Yagoro and Jisai picked up their *bokken* and squared off:

> Master Kanemaki [Jisai] decided he was going to teach his student a delicate lesson, and picked up his *bokken*. But it turned out entirely differently. Whatever he tried, Kanemaki could not break through Yagoro's defense. Each attack that he started was negated by Yagoro. In disbelief, the master picked up his wooden practice-stick for a second time, but to no avail. He even had to muster up all of his knowledge and expertise not to suffer an embarrassing defeat. Then, Yagoro lowered his *bokken*, and

bowed for [sic.] his master. He explained that he had found out that *concentrating on not losing was better than to dedicate oneself to win.** In addition, in doing so he completely went with his intuition, which made him sense when an attack was started, enabling him to take over the initiative. It was the same intuition which had saved his life in Kamekura [sic.], when someone had sneaked up to him in the dark. Yagoro described this as *isshin itto*, his sword and mind being one. Kanemaki was impressed and decided to continue to further inaugurate Yagoro in the mysteries of swordsmanship.[24]

Jisai asked Yagoro to explain his insight: "I have travelled all over the country, I have fought many *bugeisha* [martial artists], and never lost, but in this *shiai* [competition] you have shown me I can't win from you. What has happened?" Yagoro answered:

> Even when humans are asleep, when their legs are itchy they don't scratch their head. If their legs are itchy they scratch their legs, if their head is itchy they scratch their head. If there is an itchy place, their hand will reach for it. In swordsmanship it is the same if there is a *sukima* (opening or unguarded moment) my sword will go there, that is the natural instinct of humans that I have.[25]

On his own. It is unclear when Yagoro set out on his own road; some accounts suggest he stayed with Jisai for several more years, while others say that Jisai awarded him a

---

* Emphasis added. This was a point that Kotaka Sadao *Sensei* made both in person and in interviews. For example: "The most important thing for a beginner to learn in Kendo is to eliminate his fear. Do not be afraid of the opponent. Do not be worried about getting hit or losing. Get ai-uchi! [mutual strike].[22] As Kotoda Yahei Toshitada, grandson of one of Yagoro's (Ito Ittosai's) first students, put it: "In this art, the practitioner should understand the distinction between 'defeat' and 'not winning.' 'Defeat' is, first of all, [one's opponent's] winning. 'Not winning' is the situation of one's opponent's being able to defend himself. Thus, 'defeat' resides within one's self, while 'winning' resides within his opponent."[23] Sugawara (*Lives of Master Swordsmen*. Tokyo: East Publications, 1985, page 166) says Yagoro told Jisai, "To try to win is empty and to try to avoid defeat is essential."

menkyo kaiden (full licensure) and the right to establish his own school/style. In any event, before long, Yagoro set off on a *musha shugyo*, a wandering trip during which he checked out various other styles and teachers, issued and accepted challenges to matches—of which he is said to have fought 33—and either stayed to study or, more often, teach for a while. Some biographers say that once Ittosai left Jisai's school, he became ever more arrogant, rude, conceited, and tyrannical toward his students and others.

Apparently when he set off, he adopted a new name: Ito Ittosai Kagehisa (伊東 一刀斎 景久). As his "family" name, he adopted "Ito," the name of the village which had rescued and fostered him.

Ittosai's middle years. One of his first major students, possibly as early as 1578, was Kotoda Kageyuzaemon Toshinao, a retainer of the Hojo family and an experienced swordsman and expert with the spear. Toshinao combined Ittosai's teachings with his own expertise and created the first of many *ryu-ha* tracing their lineages back to Ittosai. His *Kotoda-ryu* or *Kotoda Itto-ryu*, was passed down within the family, to his son, Kotoda Jin'emon Toshishige, and eventually to his grandson, Kotoda Yahei Toshisada, who wrote the *Ittosai Sensei Kempo Sho* (*Book on Teacher Ittosai's Way of the Sword*), the first systematic exposition of Ittosai's thinking.

From the time of Toshisada, however, this style became known as *Yuishin Itto-ryu* (唯心 一刀流, "Only Heart One-Sword Style," or implicitly the "whole hearted" or "single -minded" one-sword style).* A later descendant of this school, Masaki Tadodayu Toshimitsu (1689-1776) created the *Masaki Itto-ryu* (正木一刀流).[26]

---

* Interestingly, Fujita Seiko later supposedly became the *soke*—family head, or inheritor—of this school and held a *menkyo kaiden*. On the fascinating and influential Fujita, see Christopher M. Clarke, *Okinawan Kobudo: A History of Weaponry Styles and Masters*. Huntingtown, MD: Clarke's Canyon Press, 2013, pages 127-135.

Ittosai's name

Ittosai (一刀斎) is difficult to translate into English. The first part means "one sword." This has levels of meaning, one more obvious and many deeper. On the obvious side, Ito Ittosai's style used only one sword, unlike Miyamoto Musashi's later *Nito-ryu* ("Two-sword style").

At one level, the idea of "*itto*" is that all contests must be settled with a single stroke. One characteristic of the *itto-ryu* styles is that they preempt attacks by opponents by over-riding their over-head attacks by a special use of the style's own overhead attack. But in addition to this "technical" explanation, there are deeper meanings to "*itto*."

Some of these deeper meanings were espoused by Ittosai's grand-student, Kotoda Yahei Toshisada, who left behind the closest thing there is to a *densho* or manual explaining Ittosai's style[27]:

> Our secret instruction has been that the sword and the mind are not different... Presence [i.e., the unity of mind and action] does not change with the turn of circumstances... Presence is at peace, and possesses a thousand changes; force moves, and responds to ten thousand transformations. Thus, you meet the opponent with presence, and defeat him with force. Presence and force are considered to be two, but they are one; they are considered to be one, but they are two. Force resides in presence; presence resides in force...Thus, respect the principle that arises from your own reaction, and do not generate any thinking or discrimination... Because this unification of mind does not stop with either the initial move or the follow-up it penetrates and responds to the universal principal and the ten thousand techniques...This principle is subtle and difficult to teach. It is difficult to reach by study and is, in fact, a mysterious truth transmitted from mind to mind.

This apparently is why Yagoro chose the character "*sai*" (斎), which carries a meaning of "purification" and "worship." Thus, the principle of unifying mind and action takes on and reflects the Buddhist religious principle of enlightenment, albeit manifest through the technique of the sword.

Ittosai's other personal name also has a deeper meaning. *Kage* (景, usually written 影) means a shadow, reflection, presence, or sign. *Hisa (久)* means "for a long time." This seems to suggest that Ittosai is indicating that accomplishing his principles, extracting them from the shadows and making oneself a reflection of the surroundings, is a long-term endeavor. (One writer has translated the meaning as "shadow of the roof," meaning "hidden within the brain" or mind.[28] This does not seem accurate to me.) Interestingly, the word *Kagehisa* is a homonym for "to be clouded" or "to be hidden in obscurity," a coincidence that cannot have escaped Ito Ittosai.

Around 1578, Ittosai engaged in one of his most famous matches. Visiting Misaki, a castle town at the southern end of the Miura Peninsula, not terribly far from where he had floated ashore years before, he learned that there was a Chinese ship in port. Aboard the ship was a Chinese halberdier who was going about boasting that no one could defeat him. None of the castle master's *samurai* wanted to fight the foreigner since his style and ability were a total unknown. Ittosai stepped forward, and attempting to burst the Chinese's confidence told him that "If you fight with your halberd, I'll fight with a fan."

Of course, the Chinese was incensed and insulted. The two squared off, eyeing each other warily. For a long time, they paced around each other like two giant cats looking for an opening. Finally, Ittosai threw down the fan and stood empty-handed, inviting an attack. Taken aback, the Chinese still remained wary. But eventually, he swung for Ittosai's head, hoping to cleave him from crown to groin.

Just in time, Ittosai moved inside the attack, knocked the halberd out of his opponent's hands and struck him to the ground.[28]

Around 1590, Ittosai apparently settled down somewhat and began to teach his *"Itto-ryu."* Little information is available about this portion of Ittosai's life, but he appears to have continued at least periodically wandering the country, making a living where he could by being hired by various *daimyo* to teach swordsmanship to their *samurai* on essentially short-term contracts.

At some time during his travels, Ittosai supposedly

spent an extended stay in Kyoto, the emperor's capital and the nation's seat of luxury. Here Ittosai's penchant for alcohol, women, arrogance, and challenging others to duels—sometimes to the death—almost cost him his life. According to a number of accounts, one summer he engaged in a duel with another expert—possibly Kofujita Kageyu, a master of another style and head of a *dojo*—defeating him (and probably killing him) with one stroke, his famous "*itto*."

The other teacher's students naturally were angered— Ittosai's attitude probably exacerbated their ill feelings—and decided to exact revenge. According to the legend, Ittosai was spending the night with one of his mistresses, whom the students had suborned to their plot. While the two were sleeping, the students invaded his room, armed with swords and other weapons, cut the ties to Ittosai's mosquito net so it fell around him and virtually imprisoned him, and set upon Ittosai to hack him to death.

The alarmed sword master reached next to his bed for his *katana*, but his mistress had removed it before she went to sleep. He was unarmed, surrounded, stuck in a net, and beset by a gang of swordsmen! Somehow, according to the legend, he was able to dodge and duck until he could extract himself from the net, seize a sword from one of the students, and go about disposing of the others one by one.

According to one account, Ittosai surveyed the scene of seven or eight dead *samurai*, left a letter for the police, and took to the road, thinking deeply about his own faults and their role in the near disaster.[29]

> Ittosai reflected deeply on the incident—not only on the hatred he had inspired in a number of swordsmen but on his betrayal by his mistress. He felt ashamed of himself. The incident made him realize that his narrow escape was little short of a miracle, and his boast of being a matchless and undefeated swordsman was merely vain.

> With this incident, Ittosai became a man of a different character. He no longer boasted of his talent nor used abusive language to others. Instead, he became a man of few words who did not easily put his trust in others.

Once again, he was a wanderer. However, his purpose was no longer to publicize his Itto style of swordsmanship His was a journey to tenaciously seek a genuinely worthy opponent, one skilled enough to carry on the Itto style to the next generation. But would it be possible for him to find a swordsman who could survive Ittosai's severe method of selection?[30]

This makes a wonderful modern story of sin and redemption, but it appears to be highly dubious, especially for the times and given Ittosai's final chapter.

Ittosai's unorthodox method for choosing a successor. At some time during Ittosai's wanderings, possibly after the Kyoto assassination attempt, he picked up a quite unorthodox student. Not a *samurai* at all, he was a ferryman named Zenki, who dropped his oar and decided to follow Ittosai around and master his art of the sword. By all accounts, Zenki was crude, rude, and violent. One version has the two meeting when Ittosai sought to cross a river on Zenki's ferry. Like the legend of Robin Hood and Little John, only without the good humor, Zenki is said to have rudely asked Ittosai if he was "any good" with the sword he was wearing and challenged him to a fight: Ittosai's sword against his oar. When Ittosai took up his stance, however, Zenki slowly realized he was up against a real master and backed down.

He then decided to abandon his ferry and follow Ittosai on his *musha shugyo*, studying swordsmanship from him. Even though this was before the Tokugawa shogunate's freezing of social rank, it was highly unusual for a *samurai* to accept a lowly ferry boat rower as a student. Perhaps it was a case of "birds of a feather" flocking together.

In any case, Zenki followed Ittosai, training zealously and eventually gaining a very high level of skill. A bit later, during their wanderings, Ittosai met up with a young *samurai* named Mikogami Tenzen (神子上典膳, 1560-1628), already a highly accomplished swordsman. After Ittosai completely defeated Tenzen in a challenge match, the loser begged Ittosai to allow him to become a student. Ittosai agreed and the two (or possibly three, with Zenki) resumed their wandering search for challenges and knowledge.

As Ittosai approached the age of 60, he decided it was time to decide on his successor. Logically, Zenki, his most senior and most talented student, should get that honor; Zenki certainly thought so. But Ittosai saw something in Zenki he didn't like. Perhaps it was a reflection of his own rough character; perhaps he hesitated to leave his style in the hands of an illiterate non-*samurai*. There were even intimations in some accounts that the aging Ittosai may have feared the younger Zenki.

It is not clear exactly what happened, but by some versions, Ittosai approached Tenzen and told him he wished to leave the style to him, but only if he would kill Zenki. Other versions of events suggest that Ittosai, whose character was always rough and rather cruel, decided that a fight to the death was the only way he could truly decide who was his rightful heir. In any event, he told the two that they would have to fight it out to decide who would become his successor and inherit his famous sword, the Jar-cutter.*

The two faced off: various accounts have mythologized the subsequent bout, but no one knows exactly what happened. We only know that at the end of the fight, Tenzen was standing, and the bloody corpse of Zenki lay at his feet. Ittosai is said to have given Tenzen his sword and told him to travel the country spreading the style.[31]

As for Ittosai, no one knows. Legend says that he buried Zenki at the site of the fight, then disappeared. (Some stories even hinted that Tenzen may have killed Ittosai himself.) In typical fashion, many believe Ittosai gave up swordsmanship, joined a monastery and spent another 30 years as a Zen monk.

---

* In one version, believing that Tenzen was a lesser swordsman than Zenki and would likely lose, Ittosai sought to "fix" the fight by allowing Tenzen to use his famous sword, the *Kamewari-to*.

Ito Ittosai Kagehisa

Kotaka Sadao's Version of the Founding of *Itto-ryu*

In response to questions by his students, sometime in the late 1980s or early 1990s, Kotaka Sadao wrote a seven-page (single-spaced) monograph in which he recounted the history of Ito Ittosai and the founding of *Itto-ryu* as he remembered having been told by his *sensei*, Sakurai Gennoshin Fumitaka. It contains substantial differences from the account I have put together from a wide variety of printed sources. I am including it here both to show that there are many versions of Ittosai's life and to reflect what Kotaka *Sensei* remembered after many years. As he himself acknowledged in his manuscript, "There are more than a dozen versions of *Itto-ryu* school legends. This is the story I learned from my *sensei*, Sakurai Gen'noshin Fumitaka."

[The] *Itto-ryu* school system was founded by Ito Itto-sai Kagehisa (born 1550). Itto-sai had only three lasting students or disciples in his life. Itto-sai never had his own *dojo*, but traveled all over [the] Japan[ese] Islands seeking *kendo*ists who were skilful enough to defeat him. This kind of *kendo* training is called *musha-shugyo*. *Kendo* matches for *musha-shugyo* practitioners were full-contact matches with real swords or *bokken* under the ultimate rule, life or death. One of [the] students, Kotoda Kageyu-zaemon Toshinao established himself a *kendo* school based on *Itto-ryu* principles in a small town near Kyoto. [The] remaining two students, Ono Zenki and Mikogami Tenzen Yoshiaki had followed Itto-sai's travels all over Japan Islands until Itto-sai's retirement, even though they were well [i.e., good] enough to establish their own schools anywhere in Japan, Needless to say that Itto-sai and his students were matchless *kendo*ists in Japan. They survived all the full-contact *kendo* matches with real swords and *bokken*s.

Ono Zenki's *kendo* skill was far better than that of Mikogami's. Because of Ono Zenki's sly, wicked, crude personality, Itto-sai had strong reservation to make [about making] Ono Zenki as his successor of *Itto-ryu* school. Since [the] very moment after Ono Zenki became Itto-sai's student, he tried to kill Itto-sai many times in any given day.* If he could kill Itto-sai, Ono Zenki would be the best *kendo*ist in Japan. Knowing Ono Zenki's intention,

---

* This is the only account in which I have seen such an allegation.

Itto-sai accepted him as a student and he trained Ono Zenki affectionately and sternly all the time. Itto-sai thought that living with an assassin and train[ing] him to be the best assassin, and [to] survive from [the] tenacious attacks by [his] constantly improving assassin [student] were, in turn, the best training for himself. At the same time, Itto-sai always hoped to change Ono Zenki's personality and convert him to one of the best *kendo*ists in Japan. On the other hand, Mikogami Tenzen Tadaaki was much younger than Ono Zenki and his personality was of a model *samurai*. Mikogami respected his senior student, Ono Zenki, as well as Itto-sai. Ono Zenki, being an orphan himself, treated Mikogami as his younger brother.*

Itto-sai realized that he grew [had grown] old and had to retire some day. Because of the above-mentioned reason, Itto-sai trained Ono Zenki. But, if he handed the *Itto-ryu* school to Ono Zenki, he would become an evil swordsman, a killing machine. He must get rid of Ono Zenki. Instead of killing Ono Zenki by himself, Itto-sai ordered the two students to have a real sword match to decide which one of them to succeed the *Itto-ryu* school. Only one could succeed the school and the other one should die. Itto-sai showed the sacred scroll of *Itto-ryu* school to them, placed in front of him, and told them that the victor would receive this sacred scroll and succeed the school.♦ Ono Zenki cried and said that he could not kill lovely [i.e., beloved] brother Mikogami Tenzen. Mikogami pleaded [with] Itto-sai to give the scroll to Ono Zenki because he was far more superior swordsman than he was—a senior student and elder brother. He [Zenki] would train Mikogami as one of his students and then he would hand [over] the scroll to Mikogami as his successor later.

However, Itto-sai did not listen to Ono Zenki and closed his eyes. Ono Zenki snatched the scroll and ran away. Itto-sai and Mikogami chased Ono Zenki. Ono Zenki ran into a farmer's house and hid inside the inverted huge earthenware jar used for *miso* [bean paste] fermentation with a drawn sword in his hand. Mikogami tried to flip the jar open, but Itto-sai told him not to, because Ono Zenki might sweep Mikogami's leg. Itto-sai gave his famous sword named Dotanuki◊ to Mikogami and ordered [him] to cut

---

* Available accounts other than this say almost nothing about the relationship between Mikogami and Zenki.

♦ Other accounts give a similar version, but no such scroll by Ittosai is known to have existed.

◊ Dotanuki (同田貫) is the name of a Japanese school of sword smiths from Higo province who produced swords in the *Bizen* tradition during the feudal period of Japan.

Ono Zenki together with the earthenware jar. The jar, Ono Zenki, and the scroll held in his clenched mouth were cut into two pieces. After the fight was over, Itto-sai left for the mountain range area in Western Japan. Nobody knew what became Itto-sai.

Mikogami Tenzen Tadaaki became an adopted son of Ono Zenki and changed his name to Ono Jiroemon Tadaaki when he established the first *Itto-ryu dojo* in the center of Edo (the ancient name for Tokyo).* The cut scroll and the sword (which was renamed *Kame-wari—kame* = earthenware jar, *wari* = breaker) were the symbols of (*Ono-ha*) *Itto-ryu* school successors for [the] next few hundred years. [The] whereabouts [of] the cut scroll and the sword are unknown today.

A drawing by Katsushika Hokusai (葛飾 北斎, 1760-1849) of a
duel between two warriors.

---

* It is not clear how Mikogami could have become an adopted son of Zenki
after just having killed him. For another, more standard version of how Mikogami became "Ono Tadaaki" see below.

116

Ono-ha Itto-ryu

Ittosai and Tenzen lived during the tail end of the age of war in Japan, just before Tokugawa Ieyasu finally unified the country under the rule of his family. The Tokugawa shogunate, under his successors, would last until the late 1860s, more than 250 years. By 1615, there would be no more battles to fight—and soon the shogunate would outlaw duels to the death.[32]

But that did not mean the end of swordsmanship. In fact, the Tokugawa peace fostered the development and refinement of hundreds of schools of martial arts—from *Kenjutsu* to archery, *jujutsu* to spearmanship. The House of Tokugawa would become a major sponsor of a number of martial arts masters, as would the *daimyo* (大名, great lords) who ran Japan's roughly 250 *han* (藩) or feudal domains.[33]

According to legend, during one of the trips to Edo (the capital of the Tokugawa territory before unification), by Ittosai, Mikogami Tenzen, and Zenki, Tokugawa Ieyasu offered Ittosai a position as *kenjutsu* instructor to his vassals. Ittosai wanted to continue his travel and study and declined, offering Tenzen in his place. For some reason, Ieyasu rejected the offer. (Some say that Ittosai's offer of the job to Tenzen rather than Zenki was the reason for the hard feelings that ended in the fatal duel.)

After Ittosai's death, Tenzen returned to his home region and resumed his practice as a wandering as a *ronin* (浪人, literally "floating man," a *samurai* unattached to service with a particular feudal lord). At length, he decided to return to Edo and open a swordsmanship school. On the way to Edo, an incident occurred that both speaks volumes about his temperament and that became a turning point in his life. In Hizaori, a small village near Edo, "An angry swordsman had killed a man and hid in the former's house. The villagers who were in no position to chase him out sent a messenger to Edo to plead for help."[34] The villagers called on Ieyasu and asked for help. He tasked his vassal, "Obata Kanbei Kagenori, a famous exponent of *Koshu Ryu Gungaku*" to order Tenzen to take care of the problem:

So Tenzen headed to the village and went straight to the farmhouse the swordsman was hiding in. Standing in front of the door Tenzen shouted "I am Mikogami Tenzen. I have been ordered to come here from Edo, do you want to fight me outside or shall I come in?". When the swordsman heard this he said "Often heard your name, now that I'm fortunate enough to meet you, I will come out and fight with you!" The swordsman came out and drew his long sword. In response Tenzen immediately drew his two shaku (60.60 cm) *uchigatana* [(打刀, or fighting sword] and promptly cut both arms of the opponent. Then without showing any emotion he turned to Obata and asked "Shall I cut his head?" As Obata nodded yes, Tenzen cut the swordsman's head in a single swift action. It is said Tenzen dealt with the situation in such a cold and dry manner, that onlookers watching the scene felt a shiver run over their spines. Obata reported the course of events to Tokugawa Ieyasu who then hired Mikogami Tenzen as *hatamoto* (旗本, high-level vassal) and gave him a stipend of 200 *koku* (石高).*

Joining Ieyasu's retinue. After this incident, word got back to Ieyasu about how Tenzen had conducted himself and Ieyasu hired Tenzen as a fencing instructor for his son, Hidetada (秀忠). Tenzen took on the name Ono Jiroemon Tadaaki (小野次郎右衛門忠明, 1565-1628), using his mother's maiden name and adopting the character *"tada"* from the name of Hidetada to honor his new patron.

Unfortunately, as the above story suggests, Ono, like his *sensei* and his senior, Zenki, apparently was a rather disagreeable character, not surprising, one supposes, given the company he kept and the rough life he led. This is illustrated by the story of his meeting up with, and being defeated by, Ittosai (which, naturally has several versions). All accounts seem to

---

* Japanese pay and wealth were counted in *koku*, a quantity of about 330 pounds of rice, supposedly enough to feed a person for a year, but actually short of the necessary caloric intake for a *samurai*. The wealth of feudal *han* was assessed in *koku*; the smallest was valued at 10,000 *koku*, while a very few—including the Tokugawa land holdings—were valued at over one million *koku*. The number of Tokugawa *hatamoto* varied over time but is thought to have been around 5,000. A 200 *koku hatamoto* would be a rather low-ranking one, despite the prestigious title. *Hatamoto* working directly for the family generally had incomes ranging from 100-1,000 *koku*.

agree that the then-Tenzen responded to a challenge Ittosai had posted in Tenzen's village as Ittosai was passing through on *musha shugyo*. Tenzen stepped up to the plate. According to one version, Ittosai was bending over a wood pile and as Tenzen began to draw his sword, Ittosai struck him with a stick from the pile. According to another account, Ittosai planned to use his short sword. As soon as Tenzen drew his *katana*, Ittosai disarmed him, threw Tenzen's sword on the woodpile, and stalked back into the house.

Whatever the reality, Tenzen realized he was the far inferior swordsman and stayed with Ittosai until the final duel with Zenki, eventually becoming an outstanding swordsman, but never refining his character.

This roughness carried over into his training of the future lord of the Tokugawa realm (and future *shogun*), and caused him considerable trouble:

> Tadaaki was so dedicated and strict a fencing instructor that Hidetada was never favorably disposed toward him. Once a fencing lesson began, Tadaaki made no allowance for the fact that his pupil was a son of the *shogun*. Tadaaki did not hesitate to give quick and heavy blows, and it was not unusual for Hidetada to cry out in pain. When Hidetada asked the fencing master such questions as what is the proper attitude for a swordsman, Tadaaki would give an answer implying that Hidetada was presumptuous, since his progress in swordsmanship was far from satisfactory. Therefore, it is no wonder that the fencing master earned Hidetada's enmity, and his stipend was consequently kept at a relatively low level.[35]

While in Ieyasu's service, Ono took part in several of the climactic battles of the unification of Japan, but his valor and rashness sometimes got him into further trouble. For example, at siege of Ueda Castle in 1600, Ono rushed out ahead of the other troops and was the first to strike down an enemy. While acknowledged for his bravery, he was also chastised for breaking ranks, relieved of duty, and put under temporary suspension and supervision. During the summer battles around the siege of Osaka Castle in 1615, "some fellow *hatamoto* misbehaved toward Tadaaki and caused a row. The other *hatamoto* however somehow managed to put the blame for the incident with Tadaaki, so the latter was punished yet another time. This time he was placed under house arrest."[36]

His personal conduct also caused disruption and trouble for his patron. Once, Ono supposedly went to the *dojo* of another style and made derogatory comments about their performance. The instructor confronted Ono and asked him inside to engage in a challenge duel. Ono walked through the door, pulled a stick from his belt, and struck the man between the eyes, leaving him bleeding on the floor. The fight was over before it began, but it did little to help Ono's image with officialdom.

> Another teacher came forward and said that he needed to take care of the *shihan*, and asked Tadaaki to come back the next day. Tadaaki consented, but when the next day he went back to the *dojo*, he only found a very small door open. With lightning speed he rushed in, but as the exponents of the *dojo* had covered the floor with oil, Tadaaki slipped and fell down. Some of the people of the *dojo* that were waiting inside, made symbolic cuts with their hands in his direction as a sign that this time they had managed to get him. However while Tadaaki was falling he drew his sword and swept it upwards at his opponents, he then got up and easily cut them down. It is said that since this type of behaviour from the shogun's *shihan* could not be tolerated Tadaaki was punished.[37]

By one account, Ono was banished for a time to a remote island, but somehow he always bounded back and was later brought back to Edo. After his long absence, he went to visit Hidetada, now the *shogun*. "As Tadaaki was bowing down to Hidetada, the latter said, it has been a while so let's do *tachiai**, and as he said so drew his sword. Without even as much as lifting his head, Tadaaki quickly pulled the rug the *shogun* was standing on, and made him fall down."[38]

Well, we could go on for some time about Ono and his exploits, but we would never get to *Kogen Itto-ryu*, the subject

---

* *Tachiai* is a *sumo* term for the initial clash or attack of the wrestlers. In effect, Hidetada was saying "Can you defend yourself from this unexpected attack?"

of this chapter. One more thing should be said about Ono, however. He was only one of *two* fencing instructors to the *shogun;* the other was Yagyu Tajima-no-kami Munenori, inheritor of the Yagyu style of *kenjutsu* and reputedly one of the finest swordsmen of his day. No, the two never held a match, and we can only speculate about the outcome. I suspect Ono would have come out on top, but we will never know.* Yagyu, however, was much better liked by the *shoguns* and officials at the court, and consistently received much higher stipends than Ono.[39]

Ono passes on "*Ono-ha Itto-ryu.*" "Under Tadaaki's severe guidance, excellent swordsmen were forged from among his disciples, such as Kamei Tadao; Tadaaki's younger brother, Tadanari; and Tadaaki's son, Tadatsune. All of these men later became masters of the *Itto* school or its [*Ono*-ha] branch. We can catch a glimpse of Tadaaki's severe guidance from the fact that he trained his disciples holding an iron sword with dull edges. He never used a bamboo sword for fencing practice."[41]

After Tokugawa Iemitsu, a fond lover of swordsmanship and an excellent swordsman himself, succeeded Hidetada as the third *shogun*, Tadaaki continued to serve the shogunate as a fencing instructor. But increasingly he left the instruction to his students, especially his third son and successor, Ono Jiroemon Tadatsune. Tadaaki died on November 5, 1628 leaving Tadatsune as head of both the family and the style. He became a close friend, sparring partner, and teacher to Iemitsu, the third Tokugawa *shogun*.

Ono Tadaaki had three sons, all outstanding swordsmen. The youngest, died of tuberculosis before he could establish himself or a school.[42] The second son, Ono Jiroemon Tadanari (also pronounced Chuya), opened a school outside Edo, which became known as the *Chuya-ha Itto-ryu* (忠也派一刀

---

* Reportedly, Munenori's son, Yagyu Jubei Mitsuyoshi (柳生 十兵衛 三厳, 1607–1650), did hold a friendly match with Ono, but after seeing Ono's battle -hardened will and formidable stance, he allegedly fell on his knees and declared Ono his vast superior.[40] Jubei himself would later become an enigmatic and famous figure in the history of *kenjutsu* and become a romanticized figure in popular culture up to the present day.

流) to differentiate it from the direct line of the eldest son, Tada-tsune. We will return to Tadanari and the *Chuya-ha* in a moment.

Ono-ha Itto-ryu was handed down in the family to Tadatsune, whose student, Mizoguchi Shingoemon Masakatsu created the *Mizoguchi-ha Itto-ryu* (溝口派一刀流) style, which is still in practice today. The fourth headmaster, Ono Jiroemon Tadakazu taught Tsugaru Nobumasa (津軽 信政, 1646–1710), lord of the Tsugaru clan, who established a separate line of *Ono -ha Itto-ryu*. The second lord of the Tsugaru clan, Tsugaru Tosa -no-kami Nobutoshi (c. 1720) apparently taught both Ono Tadahisa and Tadakata, descendants of Tadaaki.[43] From then on, two lines of descent taught the *Ono-ha* style: the Tsugaru and Ono branches.

Nakanishi-ha Itto-ryu

Nakanishi Chuta Tanesada studied *Ono-ha Itto-ryu* under either the fourth/fifth (Ono Jiroemon Tadakazu) or fifth/sixth (Ono Jiroemon Tadakata) generation headmaster of the style.* He established his own style, *Nakanishi-ha Itto-ryu* (中西派一刀流). The *Nakanishi-ha* is of interest to students of *Kogen Itto-ryu* principally because it was under the first and second generation (Nakanishi Chuzo Tsugutake) headmasters that protective equipment—including the *men* (helmet) and *do* (chest protector)—were first introduced. They also introduced a bamboo sparring sword (*shinai*) to replace the hardwood *bokken* that had theretofore been used in practice.

These innovations were soon spread widely, allowing students safely to conduct "full contact" matches without risk of serious injury or death.

---

* Their order number depends on whether one counts Ittosai or Ono Tadaaki as the first generation. See, Mol, *op. cit.*, pages 139-140.

Kogen Itto-ryu

As described above, the second son of Ono Tadaaki, founder of *Ono-ha Itto-ryu* and successor to Ito Ittosai, created a branch of his father's style: the *Chuya-ha Itto-ryu*. Tadanari adopted the family name "Ito" and thereafter became known as Ito Jirosuke Tadanari.* As mentioned above, "Tadanari" can also be pronounced "Chuya." He died before he could pass along his entire system or name a successor, but one of his senior students was Henma Tashiro Minamoto-no Yoshitoshi, a descendant of one of the sub-clans of the Kai Genji and of Takeda Shingen. The Henmi clan had provided one of Shingen's famous "24 Generals" and remained loyal to his ill-fated successor, Katsuyori. After Katsuyori's defeat, the Henmi family had taken up residence near the Daibosatsu Toge (大菩薩峠) or "Great Buddha Pass" through Daibosatsu Mountain (大菩薩嶺) in what is now Yamanashi prefecture.♦

The Henmi family farmed, but continued to study Shingen's *Koshu Gunkaku*, or Manual of Military Sciences, and to practice weaponry. The actual founding of their style—which became known as *Kogen Itto-ryu* (甲源一刀流剣術)—is a fascinating and unusual tale.

Sometime around 1700, a student of the Aizu region's branch of *Mizoguchi-ha Itto-ryu* named Sakurai Gosuke Naga-

---

* According to Kotaka Sadao ("Answer to the Kendo Questions"), Tadanari was adopted by his father's teacher, Ito Ittosai. I have not seen this documented elsewhere but it is entirely possible. Ittosai is not known to have left a son (at least one who was expert in *kenjutsu*) and Japanese often allowed their second, third, or subsequent sons to be adopted by heir-less friends or relatives.

♦ Mount Daibosatsu is in the Minami Alps with a marvelous view of Mount Fuji. It is a favorite weekend trip for people living in Tokyo. The pass used to be a famous section of the old Tokaido road, leading from Tokyo to Osaka. It now contains several Zen monasteries and retreats. From the 1700s to the mid—1900s it was a relatively isolated, mountainous, landlocked area surrounded by many of the highest mountains in Japan. Its central valley, the Kofu Basin, however, is quite fertile. In 1724 the area came under the direct control of the shogunate. The Henmi family became *goshi samurai*, or farmer -warriors who lived in the countryside rather than in Edo or a *daimyo*'s castle. See maps on next page.

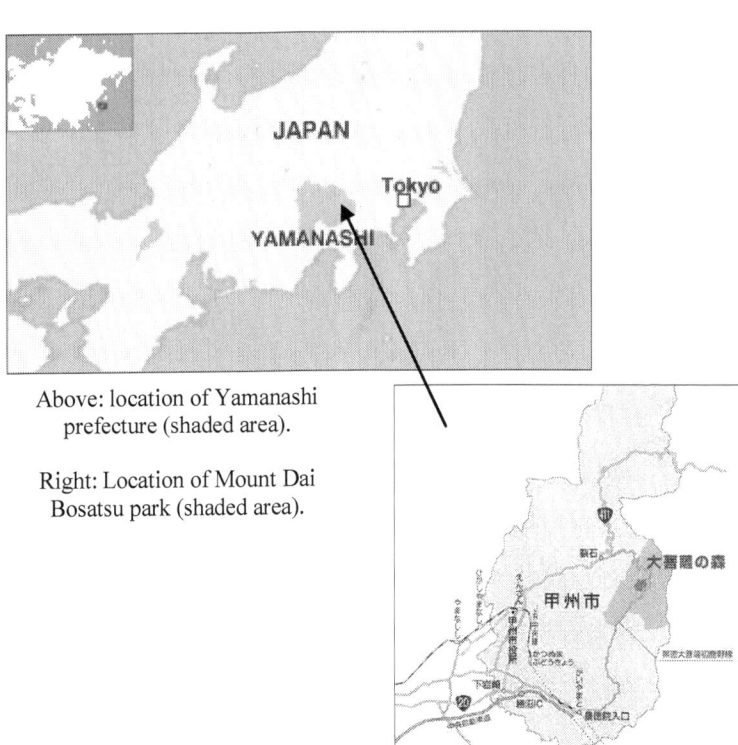

Above: location of Yamanashi
prefecture (shaded area).

Right: Location of Mount Dai
Bosatsu park (shaded area).

masa came to the Chichibu area (present-day Saitama Prefecture, bordering Yamanashi Prefecture) and taught Henmi Yoshitoshi the techniques of his style. But Sakurai* soon came to
"acknowledge the technical superiority of his erstwhile student
by later becoming a disciple of the *Kogen Itto-ryu*, accepting
Henmi as his teacher. He stayed with the Henmi family for
years, was cared for by them in his old age, and is buried in the
Henmi family cemetery near their home."[44] Thus, between
1772-1783, *Kogen Itto-ryu* emerged as a combination of the
Henmi family style of *kenjutsu*, the *Mizoguchi-ha Itto-ryu* of
Sakurai, and the military arts inherited from Takeda Shingen,
which included various weapons other than the sword, battlefield strategy, tactics, horseback riding, swimming (with and
without armor), and other war-related knowledge.[45]

---

* Sakurai Gosuke Nagamasa was an ancestor of the Sakurai Gennoshin Fumitaka with whom Kotaka Sadao studied in the immediate post-World War II
period. Thus the relationship between the Henmi and Sakurai families appears
to have endured over several centuries.

The name of the style is derived from the character for "Kai," (甲) the province of the Takeda clan in present-day Yamanashi prefecture, and "Gen," (源) the first character of the Genji (or, in its alternate pronunciation, Minamoto) clan. Most Japanese pronounce the combination as Kogen (or Kohgen), but Kotaka Sadao in his later years used the pronunciation "Kaigen" to differentiate it from the Henmi family style.

The *Kogen Itto-ryu* was passed down from Henmi Tashiro Minamoto-no Yoshitoshi (1746-1828) through eight descendants in the family to the current 9th generation *soke*, Henmi Chifuji, a well-respected master. He remains little known to the outside world because he continues to keep the style relatively insular and teaches in the family's original 200 year old *dojo*, which measures perhaps some 50 by 15 feet.[46] According to one individual who has visited the school:

An old *kago* (palanquin) is kept up in the rafters. Old farming equipment (some of it for silkworm cultivation) is also stored there. A large door leads in from the earthen courtyard. As one looks toward the "front" of the *dojo*, there is a small raised *shihan shitsu* (room for the teachers) off to the left, covered with straw mats; in that room is an image of Marishiten,* to which members of the *dojo* bow at the beginning and end of training. A couple of spears and *naginata*, used for special demonstrations, are kept over the door of the *shihan shitsu*; otherwise, trainees bring their own equipment with them and nothing is left at the *dojo*.[47]

The *Kogen Itto-ryu* was a well-known style in the 19th century, and had spread its teaching over much of northern and

---

* Marishiten is a Buddhist *deva* or *bodhisattva* associated with light and the sun. An important deity in the esoteric Shingon and Tendai schools, Marishiten was adopted by the *samurai* as early as the 8th century as a protector and patron. Worship of Marishiten, like the much later practice of Zen meditation, is supposed to free the *samurai* from interest in the issues of victory or defeat (or life and death), thus allowing transcendence to a level where he becomes so empowered that he is freed from his own concern about mortality. The end result is that he becomes a better warrior. This worship was also to provide a way to achieve selflessness and compassion through Buddhist training by incorporating a passion for the mastery of the self. See, for example, David A. Hall, *The Buddhist Goddess Marishiten: A Study of the Evolution and Impact of her Cult on the Japanese Warrior.* Netherlands: Global Oriental 2013.

western parts of current-day Musashi province northeast of Tokyo. As a prominent school, it occasionally faced challenges by other schools or visiting swordsmen on *musha shugyo*. One such challenge was by the *Shinto Munen-ryu dojo* of Togasaki Kumataro Teruyoshi in Kiyoku Village in Saitama District.

Cameron Hurst tells the story:

It was on the sixteenth day of the first month of 1836 that Hemmi [Henmi] Taishiro Nagahide, nephew of Hemmi Yoshitaka [the head of the school], met the *Shinto munen-ryu* instructor Okawa Heibei Hidekatsu in a famous match. Okawa, then thirty-five, ran his own *dojo* in Yokonuma within the Kawagoe domain. Receiving his *menkyo* certification from Akiyama Masatake in 1820, when he was only twenty years old, Okawa was the head of a prosperous *dojo*. But he was surrounded by two growing *Kogen itto-ryu dojo*. Angered at the local popularity of *Kogen itto-ryu*, Okawa determined to display his superiority and that of his school by smashing the reputation of the senior *Kogen itto-ryu* fencer, Hemmi Yoshitaka and his *Yobukan dojo*.

Arriving by palanquin at the *Yobukan dojo* in the predawn hours, Okawa waited until sunrise, knocked on the gate, and announced himself. Aware that the Hemmi head had accepted the challenge, several hundred students and neighbors gathered anxiously at the *dojo* to watch. Expecting to see Hemmi Yoshitaka take on Okawa, the onlookers were shocked to see his nephew, Nagahide, stride into the *dojo* carrying his *shinai*. Though only nineteen, he was more than six feet tall and had a magnificent physique.

The two bowed formally to each other, and Nagahide addressed Okawa: "In our *ryu* we strike to the chest, so please wear your *do* [chest protector]." But the confident Okawa, indignant at having to fight a mere youth, disdained any such protection and prepared to fence.

The two swordsmen focused intently on one another in the hushed *dojo*. Nagahide lunged forward with two successive throat-level "two-handed thrusts" (*morote-zuki*), a secret *Kogen itto-ryu* technique, which Okawa avoided by backing away skillfully. But just when Nagahide seemed about to deliver a third thrust, he suddenly dropped his *shinai* and struck straight into the chest. Okawa dropped to the floor, spitting blood.

The *Yobukan* students were ecstatic over Nagahide's victory, and Nagahide came to be called the "Little Goblin of Chichibu" (*Chichibu no ko-tengu*). His reputation soared, and students flocked to the *dojo*. The victory was considered so important that from then on, the *dojo* commenced its New Year practice on the sixteenth of the first month, in commemoration of Nagahide's victory.

Okawa, for his part, recovered from his injury in several months, then devoted himself to learning the strengths and weaknesses of the *Kogen itto-ryu*—especially how to defend against the blow that had felled him. Six months later, when he felt that he had found a solution, he challenged a local *Kogen itto-ryu* fencer named Fukuoka Honnosuke, a Hemmi student who administered a large *dojo* of his own. Both fencers wore complete protective gear for the match. This time Okawa had prepared himself well, and when Fukuoka's thrust came at his throat, he parried the blow and struck Fukuoka's mask for a clear victory. Even though Fukuoka's *dojo* was only a minor branch of the *Kogen itto-ryu*, Okawa had still won a victory over that school. His honor was restored, his fame rose throughout the region, and *Shinto munen-ryu* students swelled in number. Such was the nature of fencing competition in Tokugawa Japan.[48]

The Henmi family's *Kogen Itto-ryu dojo.*

127

Technical Characteristics of *Kogen Itto-ryu*

"There are twenty-five sword techniques in *Kogen Itto-ryu* and five *naginata waza*, which were introduced from the *Toda-ha Buko-ryu*. That may not seem like a very large technical repertoire, but the content of the techniques is so well-conceived and executed that any more would be extraneous.

Although the *iaijutsu* techniques are no longer practiced, their names remain in the *mokuroku* and deserve mention because of their unusual nature. Unlike any other *ryu*, the *iai* techniques are referred to by the various *kuji* (literally, "nine characters") derived from esoteric Buddhism, and are used by *koryu* in various ways to instill particular mental states that are useful in combat and in training. Each of the characters is associated with a particular Buddhist value, but detailed information about the techniques is not available. Most current members of the *Kogen itto-ryu* are skilled exponents of *Muso Shinden-ryu iaido* and *kendo*, as well as the classical techniques; some also have backgrounds in *jojutsu* or other modern unarmed arts.

The *Kogen Itto-ryu* technique is very spare with an economy of movement and a very strict sense of "line" and "timing." It has no superfluous content, although the meaning or utility of some movements is not immediately apparent. The *reiho* (formal etiquette) of the *ryu* is also fairly unique and seems to be a development of the mid-Edo period in that a *tachi-ainin* (observer) lays out the weapons and stays in attendance throughout the performance of techniques, a holdover from dueling etiquette."

Source: "Kogen Itto-ryu" at http://en.allexperts.com/e/k/ko/kogen_itto-ryu.htm. Photo: Practice at the *Kogen Itto-ryu Honbu Dojo.*

Kotaka Sadao on *Itto-ryu* and *Kogen Itto-ryu*

(The following two descriptions were posted on the website of Kotaka Sadao's United States Classical Kendo Federation. The website is no longer active. These appear to be from 1997-1999.)

Kogen Itto-ryu Kenjutsu

"Learn by being cut." This rather strange advice gives an example of this harsh swordsman's character. Unlike many sword experts of his day, Ittosai attached little mystical belief in swordsmanship or its techniques. Although not totally mechanical, the Itto ryu has the reputation of being one of the most technique oriented of the classical sword schools. Ittosai received his formal training from Kanemaki Kanemaki [*sic.*, Jisai] of the Chujo Ryu. After less than five years of training, Ittosai announced that he had reached a full understanding of the underlying principles of swordsmanship, then backed it up by defeating Kanemaki in a series of practice matches. He then began one of his many wandering trips to polish his techniques. The main idea of the Itto ryu is that one technique can be expanded in a countless number. Central to Ittosai's idea of swordsmanship was that of the attitude of not losing. Instead of striving for victory, a swordsman, according to Ittosai, should concentrate on not losing. Proper timing and the training to be able to apply proper timing is critical to this idea. The key technique to the Itto ryu is kiri-otoshi. This could also be called an opposition cut because the technique itself makes a counter cut which deflects an attacker's cut, all in one motion. The advantage of timing this idea gives over an opponent has to be seen to be understood. Parry counterattack and defeat of the opponent all take place in an instant in one stroke of the sword. Itto Ittosai was one of the few kenjutsu masters to face a martial artist [from] outside of Japan.

A brief history of Kogen Itto Ryu

The founder of Kogen Itto-ryu, Hennmi Tashiro Yoshitoshi is the direct descendant of Takeda of Hennmi (one of Takeda Shingen's younger brothers). My ancestor of that time is Takeda of Hajikano (one of Takeda Shingen's younger brothers). Both Hennmi [Henmi] and Hajikano are the name of cities where strategically important border defense forts for Lord Takeda's fief were located. Since Takeda Shingen became the Supreme Commander of unified Kai Genji clan, in order to clear the line of command, the name Takeda is used by Shingen himself and the first son of Shingen's direct descendants. Thus, all Shingen's younger brothers have changed their names, for example, Takeda of Hennmi (castle; at that time the fort developed to a castle) to Hennmi, Takeda of Hajikano (castle) to Hajikano, Takeda of Yamanashi changed to Yamanashi (my mother's ancestor).

Following the similar tradition, [the] Kotakari clan branched out from [the] Hajikano clan. [The] Kotaka clan branched out from [the] Kotakari clan.

Takeda Shingen published many arts of war books, so called Koshu-ryu Arts of War and Takeda's War Strategy, Takeda's War Management that were effectively used [during the] very last stage of [the] Pacific War. The military training and education of [the] Kai-genji Army under Shingen's command are one of the best in the world.

The Kogen (which is the contraction of Kai Genji) Itto-ryu founder, Hennmi Tashiro Yoshitoshi, who learned Chuya-ha Ittoryu from Sakurai Nagamasa (my *sensei* Sakurai Gen'noshin Fumitaka's ancestor), incorporated some parts of Kai-genji military training including *yari* techniques into Itto-ryu swordsmanship.

Itto-ryu Lineage

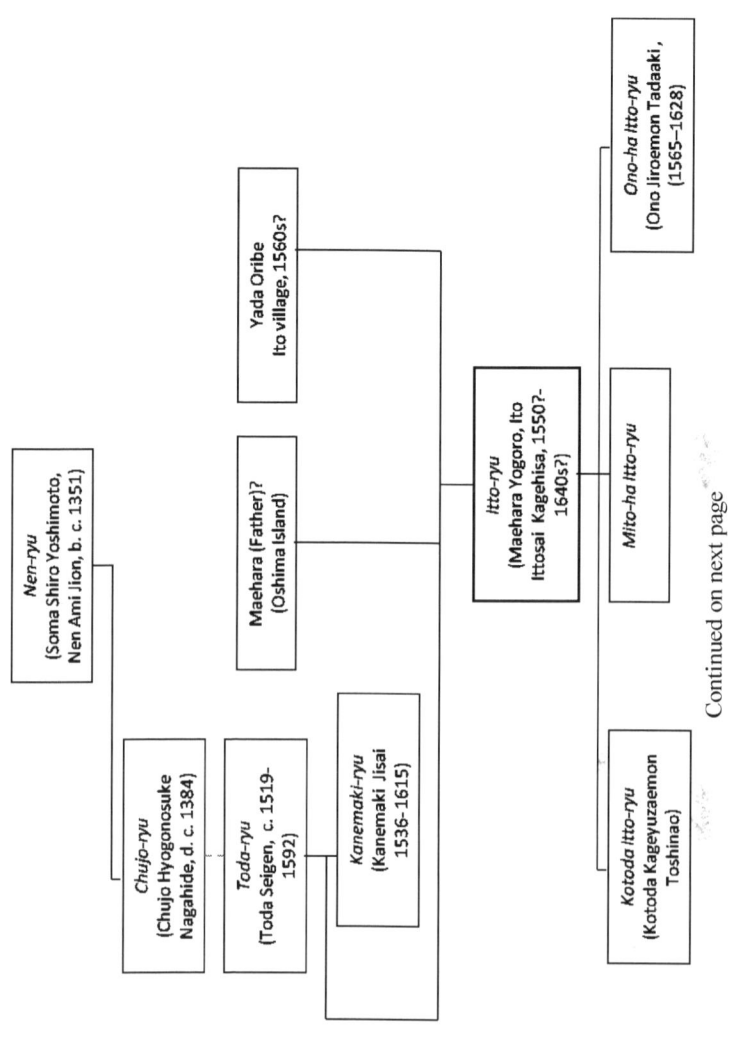

Nen-ryu
(Soma Shiro Yoshimoto,
Nen Ami Jion, b. c. 1351)

Chujo-ryu
(Chujo Hyogonosuke
Nagahide, d. c. 1384)

Toda-ryu
(Toda Seigen, c. 1519-
1592)

Kanemaki-ryu
(Kanemaki Jisai
1536-1615)

Yada Oribe
Ito village, 1560s?

Maehara (Father)?
(Oshima Island)

Itto-ryu
(Maehara Yogoro, Ito
Ittosai Kagehisa, 1550?-
1640s?)

Mito-ha Itto-ryu

Kotoda Itto-ryu
(Kotoda Kageyuzaemon
Toshinao)

Ono-ha Itto-ryu
(Ono Jiroemon Tadaaki,
(1565-1628)

Continued on next page

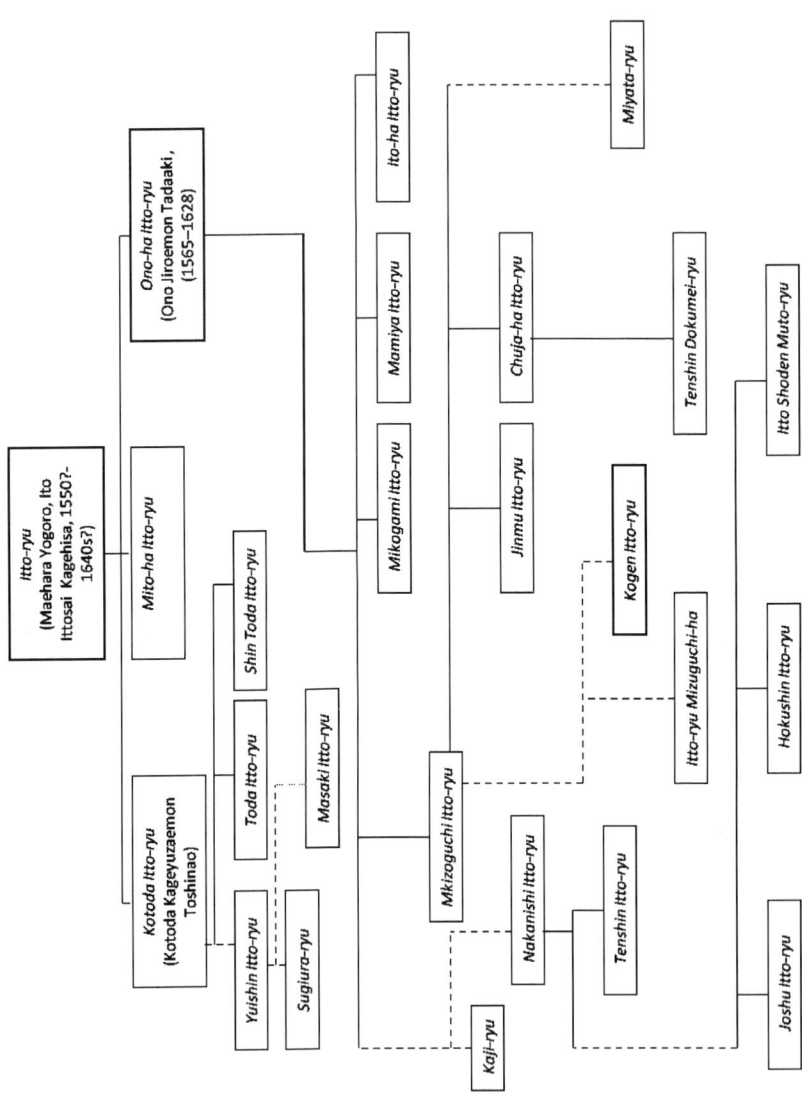

The following entries appear in the lineage chart:

- Itto-ryu (Maehara Yogoro, Ito Ittosai Kagehisa, 1550?-1640s?)
- Ono-ha Itto-ryu (Ono Jiroemon Tadaaki, 1565-1628)
- Mito-ha Itto-ryu
- Kotoda Itto-ryu (Kotoda Kageyuzaemon Toshinao)
- Itto-ha Itto-ryu
- Miyata-ryu
- Mamiya Itto-ryu
- Chuja-ha Itto-ryu
- Tenshin Dokumei-ryu
- Mikogami Itto-ryu
- Jinmu Itto-ryu
- Kogen Itto-ryu
- Itto Shoden Muto-ryu
- Shin Toda Itto-ryu
- Toda Itto-ryu
- Masaki Itto-ryu
- Mkizoguchi Itto-ryu
- Itto-ryu Mizuguchi-ha
- Hokushin Itto-ryu
- Yuishin Itto-ryu
- Sugiura-ryu
- Nakanishi Itto-ryu
- Tenshin Itto-ryu
- Kaji-ryu
- Joshu Itto-ryu

Kotaka Sadao's "Sakurai-ha Kogen Itto-ryu" and the Shinsengumi

Overleaf: Kotaka Sadao engaging in meditation before class at the Covington, KY *karate dojo* of *Hanshi* William Dometrich. Photo courtesy of Hisako Kotaka.

This chapter will discuss two main issues: first, the chaotic times of the late 1850s-late 1860s during which Kotaka *Sensei*'s style was battle tested repeatedly in the internal wars, disturbances, and lawlessness that eventually gave birth to the Meiji Restoration, and second, the origins, lineage, and legitimacy of "*Sakurai-ha Kogen Itto-ryu.*"

The period around the Meiji Restoration is an extraordinarily complex period in Japanese history, with numerous important actors, great controversy about who were the "good guys" and who were the "bad guys," lots of changing of sides, and much betrayal, violence, and brutality, all of which eventually produced the demise of the 250-year-old shogunate, the restoration of power to the emperor (and, mostly, to his close advisors), and the beginning of the modernization of Japan.[1] This period set Japan on the road that would end in the Second World War, utter defeat, and rebirth as a modern, peaceful nation.

This was the period and environment through the end of which Dr. Kotaka's teacher lived. It heavily informed Kotaka *Sensei*'s view of history—he was, for example, an unabashed supporter of the often denigrated Shinsengumi, a pro-shogunate irregular police force that fought numerous duels and battles, engaged in assassinations, and ultimately was defeated and outlawed. Most of its leaders were either killed in battle, took their own lives, or ended up in prison. Kotaka's own teacher reportedly narrowly avoided such a fate, spared perhaps because he was one of the youngest members of the group. An apparent supporter of the political right-wing, Kotaka's instructor was also sought out by the U.S. and Allied Occupation forces after World War II. As a result, he kept a low profile and destroyed many of his historical documents, making it all but impossible to reconstruct accurately his history, actions, and sword style during the turbulent period from the 1860s-1945.

This chapter will begin with a very brief historical background to the period before and during the Meiji Restoration—we can only touch the surface of this very complex period—and will conclude with some observations on why the *Sakurai-ha Kogen Itto-ryu* is virtually unknown and is significantly different from the Henmi family's *Kogen Itto-ryu.*[2]

The Shinsengumi: *Kenjutsu* During Turbulent Times

T o better understand the mentality of Kotaka *Sensei* and his *Sakurai-ha Kogen Itto-ryu*, it is helpful to understand the background of the times and the role of the Shinsengumi. In 1853, U.S. Navy Commodore Matthew Perry abruptly shoved open the door to Japan, waking the country from nearly 250 years of isolation and shocking its leaders by exposing its weakness and military backwardness. Initially, *all* factions in Japanese politics wanted to "expel the barbarians," but they gradually separated into three general camps, with each camp riven by personal, family, and factional interests, disagreements, ambitions, and hatreds.

- One camp, which became known as "**Loyalists**," rallied around the xenophobic Emperor Komei, who was sequestered in his isolated imperial palace in Kyoto. Their rallying cry became "*Sonno Joi*," or "Revere the Emperor, Expel the Barbarians." They concluded that the shogunate, which was being constantly pressed and brow-beaten by foreign diplomatic and military officials, was incapable of protecting the country, was too willing to accommodate foreign interests by signing trade treaties (especially because they failed to get imperial ratification), open ports to foreign ships, accept loans from foreign governments, and otherwise allow Japan to be "disrespected" and pushed around by foreigners. They called on the shogun, Iemochi, to turn over (actually "return") power to the emperor and restore him to the position of both reigning and ruling. (In practice, of course, this meant that his most important *daimyo* and Court supporters would exercise real power.) The Loyalists assumed the name "*Shishi*," or "Men of High Purpose."
- The second major camp was the *Bakufu*, or shogunate itself. While they also wanted to "expel the barbarians," they sought to protect the rule of

Emperor Komei   Shogun Tokugawa Yoshinobu

the House of Tokugawa and to strengthen Japan by acquiring Western military equipment, adopting Western military methods, drastically curbing the semi-independent authority of the *daimyo*, and reestablishing a strong Tokugawa authoritarian government.

- A third camp wanted to secure the independence of Japan by creating a ***Union of Court and Camp*** (i.e., *Bakufu*), cementing the relationship by the marriage of an imperial princess to the Tokugawa shogun.

A bold assassination. The Tokugawa, at first, continued to hold the upper hand. They appointed a strong, dictatorial, and much-disliked regent for the mentally handicapped and medically fragile shogun, Iesada: Lord Ii Naosuke. Regent Ii arranged for the young lord of Kii, one of two main candidates, to succeed Iesada, who died soon after. The young *daimyo* of Kii now became the fourteenth Shogun, Tokugawa Iemochi, in whose name Regent Ii negotiated a commercial treaty with the United States. Because he did so without Imperial sanction, the Loyalists were infuriated.

On a snowy morning, March 3, 1860, 18 swordsmen from the *han* (feudal provinces) of Mito and Satsuma—who were members of the Loyalist party—waylaid Regent Ii's palanquin outside the Sakurada Gate, a main entrance to the shogun's Edo Castle, and assassinated him. This brought an abrupt end to Ii's reign of terror, but unleashed a wave of assassinations that would not end until after the downfall of the *Bakufu* seven years later.

The main opponents of the *Bakufu* were the domains farthest from Edo—especially the Satsuma, Choshu, and Tosa—which had never really been conquered by Tokugawa Ieyasu when he set up the Tokugawa shogunate in the years after 1600 and which had remained largely autonomous since then. Members of these clans became among the most influential advisors and strongest supporters of the imperial court in Kyoto.

The effort to "Unite Court and Camp" through the wedding between the young shogun and the princess which took place in December 1861, failed to calm xenophobic and anti-shogunate sentiment throughout Japan:

> By the summer of 1862, hordes of *ronin*—renegade *samurai* who had fled their clans to fight for the Loyalist cause—had gathered in Kyoto. The formerly tranquil Imperial capital

Yoshitoshi Taiso's depiction of the assassination of Ii Naosuke.

was now transformed into a sea of blood. Loyalists crying "Heaven's Revenge" drew their lethal swords on the enemies of their cause, as murder of Tokugawa supporters became a daily occurrence.[3]

Recruiting a *ronin army*. Having promised to "expel the barbarians," but having accomplished nothing toward that end, Shogun Iemochi was summoned to Kyoto to explain in person to the emperor why he had not fulfilled his promise. "This visit was a precedent breaking event—not since the third Shogun of the Tokugawa Bakufu, Tokugawa Iemitsu, had a reigning shogun gone to Kyoto."[4]

In order to protect the emperor during his overland travel from Edo to Kyoto and while he was in the hostile imperial capital, the *Bakufu*, officials of the *Bakufu* decided to recruit a corps of *ronin*, (浪人, "wave men")—*samurai* who had either deserted their hereditary lords or were left leaderless by the death of their lord (or *roshi*, 浪士, "floating warriors," as they preferred to be called).

To recruit and command this corps, the *Bakufu* turned to Kiyokawa Hachiro, a renowned swordsman of the *Hokushin Itto-ryu* and graduate of the famed *Chiba Dojo*, one of the three most prestigious fencing schools in Edo. Helping him with the recruitment effort was the assistant instructor of the *Chiba Dojo*, Yamaoka Tesshu, who would later become one of the most famous swordsmen of his time.[5] Kiyokawa's small army of about 250 men—called the *Roshigumi*, or Group of Masterless Warriors"— which guarded the shogun on the 300 mile journey, arrived in Kyoto in mid-February.

Chiba Shusaku Nairmasa
(千葉 周作 成政,
1793-1856)
Head of the Chiba *Kenjutsu Dojo.*

But the *Bakufu* had badly miscalculated: Kiyokawa was actually not a Tokugawa supporter, but a staunch Loyalist:

139

No sooner had they arrived at [the village of] Mibu [outside Kyoto] than Kiyokawa assembled all 250 men into the cramped confines of the main building at their temple headquarters. The men seated themselves on the tatami-covered floor before the Buddhist altar, swords placed at their sides. Kiyokawa stood at the altar facing the assembly. Suddenly and in no uncertain terms he declared, eyes flashing, that men of high purpose must place their true loyalty with the emperor and not with the Tokugawa. The corps had been recruited for their loyalty and patriotism, he reminded them. Their actual purpose for coming to Kyoto had not been to protect the shogun, but rather to help Iemochi fulfill his promise to expel the foreigners. Kiyokawa now presented his men with a letter addressed to the Imperial Court, expressing these views and offering up the "loyal and patriotic" corps as an army of Sonno-Joi.[6]

The shogunate quickly recalled Kiyokawa and his *ronin* to Edo, but a small group of its members refused to return. Most were from the Tokugawa strongholds of Mito, Musashi, or Edo, and were loyal to the shogun. Of them 13, were adamant about remaining to guard that *Bakufu* and expel the foreigners. The Tokugawa government had appointed Matsudaira Katamori, the *daimyo* of Aizu *han* and a collateral member of the Tokugawa clan, to serve as "Military Commissioner of Kyoto"—and protector of Tokugawa interests in the fractious imperial capital.[7]

Katamori quickly hired the 13 former members of the *Roshigumi*, renaming the group the *Shinsengumi*, or "Newly Selected Corps." They proceeded to recruit additional *roshi*, eventually expanding the Shinsengumi to between 250-300 men.[8]

The Shinsengumi. The group was initially headed by two extremely powerful swordsmen—and bitter rivals.

- **Kondo Isamu** (or Isami, 近藤 勇, 1834-1868) was born to a relatively well-off peasant family under the name Miyagawa Katsugoro in a village in Musashi province. An avid reader of the emerging genre of historical novels of derring-do, he enrolled at the *Shieikan*, the main *dojo* of the *Tennen Rishin-ryu* style of swordsman-

新
選
組

Shinsen-gumi

140

ship.[9] A very promising student, he was adopted by the *dojo*'s head, Kondo Shusuke. On September 30, 1861, Katsugoro became the fourth generation master of *Tennen Rishin-ryu*, assuming the name Kondo Isamu and taking charge of the *Shieikan*. In 1862, Kondo was one of the candidates for a *kenjutsu* teaching position at the *Kobusho*, the shogunate's newly established military school. He never joined the school, however, because he was recruited for the *Roshigumi*.*

Kondo Isamu

---

* - Kondo's name is sometimes given as "Isami," an alternate pronunciation. Dr. Kotaka said that in his region, Kondo's name was always pronounced "Isamu."

- The other Shinsengumi leader was **Serizawa Kamo** (芹沢 鴨, 1826?-1863), a psychopathic killer, sadist, drunkard, and rapist. He was from a low-level *samurai* family in Mito and was a high-level expert in the *Shinto Munen-ryu* (神道無念流) *kenjutsu*.*

Serizawa Kamo

* Technically there were three co-captains, the third being Niimi Nishigi (or Shinmi Nishiki, 新見 錦, 1836-1863), but Niimi—also a master of *Shinto Munen-ryu*—played a small role. Niimi was found guilty of extorting money for use at the geisha houses and was forced to submit *seppuku* in 1863.

Some of Serizawa Kamo's Crimes

Serizawa was the "pampered youngest son of a wealthy, low-ranking samurai family of Mito Han...he stood tall and erect—an excessively proud man, well built and endowed with extraordinary physical strength. As if to flaunt his strength, he carried a heavy iron-ribbed fan, with which he threatened to pummel men who got in his way. Engraved on his weapon-fan were eight Chinese characters which read, "Serizawa Kamo, loyal and patriotic samurai."

Before joining the Roshigumi, Serizawa was a member of the Tengu-to, and extremist anti-foreign group, and was in charge of about 300 men. He supposedly taught swordsmanship to the group's leader, Takeda Kouunsai. It was rumored that he had punished several wrongdoers within the group by severing their fingers, hands, noses, or ears. He is said to have beheaded three of his men after they quarreled in their headquarters. When he went to the sacred Kashima Shrine, holy especially to swordsmen, where he complained that a shrine drum was too big and ripped it with his fan. Shogunate officials arrested him and sentenced him to death for the three murders, but he was reprieved to join the Roshigumi. Unfortunately, he quickly resumed his erratic and violent behavior in Kyoto.*

- On the way to Kyoto, he set fire to the inn where the group was staying when Kondo inadvertently forgot to reserve him a room.
- He raped the wife of a textile merchant in Kyoto to whom he owed money.
- He extorted money from numerous businesses under threats.
- When crossing a small bridge, he ran into a *sumo* wrestler and abruptly ordered him aside. When the wrestler demurred, Serizawa pulled his short sword and struck the man down. Later that night, a group of about 20-30 of the wrestler's friends attempted to exact revenge. Serizawa and seven of his comrades cut them to ribbons, killing five and sending the rest off injured.
- In June, Serizawa, while drunk again, smashed up the Sumiya restaurant in Shimabara, after attacking the estate of an official from Minakuchi who had complained about "certain *roshi*" and their behavior.
- In 1863 his group destroyed the Yamatoya silk store with a cannon, when the staff members wouldn't hand over cash.[10]

* On Serizawa possibly suffering from syphilis, see Hillsborough, *Shinsengumi*, page 32.

Appendix C contains information on a number of other Shinsengumi leaders, members, and martial arts instructors, and their exploits need not detain us here. Suffice it to say that Serizawa committed so many crimes that people began to change the nickname of the group from the *Miburoshi* (壬生浪士, "Warriors from Mibu," a suburb of Kyoto where they stayed) to the *Miburoshi* (狼浪士, "Wolves of Mibu") because of their depredations. Finally, Katamori—the "protector" of Kyoto—and Kondo had had enough.

On either the night of September 16 or 18, 1863—the records are unclear—Kondo held a party for Serizawa and some of his subordinates and followers. Plying him with copious *sake*, he sent Serizawa and two colleagues home in a palanquin. When they reached home, they dallied with pleasure girls and continued drinking. Kondo's right-hand man, Hijikata Toshizo (土方 歳三), stayed with them, making sure they were completely inebriated. When the three fell asleep, Hijikata and Okita Soji (沖田 総司, probably the best swordsman in the whole Corps) killed Serizawa and one of his men.

> The next day Kondo issued an official report to Lord Matsudaira Katamori, stating that Serizawa and Hirayama had been killed in their sleep by unknown assassins. Their funeral at Mibu Temple...was a solemn occasion befitting their positions in the Shinsengumi. The coffins of the two men were laid side by side. Their wounds were wrapped with white cotton cloth. Their wooden practice swords were placed at their sides. The corpses were formally dressed in wide trousers and jackets adorned with their respective family crests. In attendance were all of the corps-men, including Kondo and the four assassins.[11]

With Kondo and his right-hand man, Hijikata Toshizo, now completely in charge of the Shinsengumi, the group proceeded to viciously crack down on trouble-makers and to fight against Loyalists, as the *Bakufu* attempted to push back the rising tide of efforts at imperial restoration. After a brutal interrogation of a captured Loyalist *samurai* by Hijikata, the Shinsengumi discovered that a group of Loyalist *ronin* who were causing considerable chaos in Kyoto were using the Ikedaya (池田屋) Inn as their headquarters.

On July 8, 1864, Kondo led a night-time assault against

the Loyalists. A total of eight *shishi* (Loyalists) were killed and twenty-three arrested; the Shinsengumi lost only one member in the battle, though two more members would later die of injuries. The later captain of the first Shinsengumi unit, Okita Soji collapsed during the affair, apparently as a result of the tuberculosis which eventually killed him at the age of 25. This was one case where the Shinsengumi indisputably did something good for Japan; the *Shishi* (Loyalist) plotters were planning to burn down Kyoto and kidnap the emperor.[12]

Hijikata Toshizo, "Demon Vice Commander" of the Shinsengumi

Further details of the Shinsengumi's activities need not detain us excessively; these incidents give a sufficient impression of the violent and dangerous life they led. When full-scale war broke out between the Imperial Loyalists and the supporters of the shogunate (the "Boshin War"), nearly 100 members of the Shinsengumi died at the January 1868 Battle of Toba-Fushimi. The shogun's forces suffered a major defeat, and members of the Shinsengumi retreated along with other Tokugawa partisans, losing a series of battle. Kondo was captured shortly thereafter and was beheaded as a criminal on May 17, 1868. Okita died not long after of tuberculosis, Hijikata was wounded in mid-May, but escaped, only to die at the climactic Battle of Hakodate in May 1869. This effectively was the end of the Shinsengumi;

Okita Soji (沖田 総司)

145

only a few members survived to surrender. A number of its lower-ranking members had melted away during the previous year and, after keeping a low profile for some time, resumed normal lives, although the days of the *samurai* were largely over.

I would be remiss, however, in moving on before describing the draconian discipline and strict *bushido* code of the Shinsengumi (see Appendix D), a code that undoubtedly followed those members who survived the destruction of the Corps to their graves. In the words of the premier English-language author and historian of the times:

> It is said that more men of the Shinsengumi were killed for violating the corps' draconian code than died in battle. The number of victims of the code is unknown. Of the twenty-two of the corps' most noted officers, six were assassinated by their own men, three were ordered to commit *seppuku* for violating the code, two were executed, and only three survived the revolution. One of the survivors erected a stone monument for the repose of the souls of his dead comrades. Engraved in this monument are the names of sixty-five men, many victims of the code...[13]

But what of the connection of *Sakurai-ha Itto-ryu* to the Shinsengumi, as claimed by Dr. Kotaka?

Sakurai-ha Kogen Itto-ryu

D r. Kotaka's claims to have taught *"Kogen Itto-ryu"* were disputed by the small group of *Kogen Itto-ryu* practitioners connected to those still in Japan, a few of their foreign students, and a number of web forum posters who had never met him. Dr. Kotaka reported that his main instructor was Sakurai Gen'noshin Fumitaka. This Sakurai was a direct descendant of the Sakurai Gosuke Naga-masa of the *Mizoguchi-ha Itto-ryu* who joined the Henmi family; the subsequent style of *Kogen Itto-ryu* was the product of an exchange of ideas.

According to information passed on by Dr. Kotaka, two branches of *Kogen Itto-ryu* emerged, the *"Henmi-ha,"* headed by the Henmi family which is now in its 9th generation as leaders of the style, and a *"Hiruma-ha,"* founded by Hiruma Yohachi (Toshiyuki), who broke away from the purely *kata*-oriented approach of the Henmi family to adopt the newly introduced *bogu* and full-contact *shinai kendo* introduced by Nakanishi Chuzo (mid-18th century), the founder of *Nakanishi-ha Itto-ryu*, as well as the full range of combat oriented fighting techniques.[14] At some point, the "Hiruma" branch of *Kogen Itto-ryu* disappeared, but a compilation of the "100 Greatest Swordsmen" of Japan included three members of the Hiruma family (in positions 69-71), likely relatives of Yohachi.[15]

Fighting styles of the Shinsengumi. The *Hiruma-ha Kogen Itto-ryu*, according to Dr. Kotaka, was one of the two main styles studied by the Shinsengumi swordsmen, though I can find no corroboration of that assertion. The main styles taught and used by Shinsengumi leaders and *kenjutsu* instructors were the:

- *Tennen Rishin-ryu* (天然理心流), created by Kondo Kuranosuke Nagahiro around 1789. This style was popularized by Kondo Shusuke Kunitake (近藤周助 邦武 1792-1867), the third generation master of the style, who, together with Sato Hikogoro (佐藤彦五郎), spread its practice throughout the farming population of the Tama rural district of western Tokyo. Since the first and second generation masters each adopted a student with superb skills to be the next master, in 1849 the childless Kondo Shusuke decided to adopt a sixteen-year-old student named Miyagawa Katsugoro, who later changed his name to Kondo Isamu (近藤 勇), one of the main leaders of the Shinsengumi.
- The *Shinto Munen-ryu* (神道無念流), founded by

---

* The predominance of these styles is attested to in the table on the pages 149-150, showing the style and ranking of each of the major Shinsengumi figures and who were its chief *kenjutsu* instructors.

Fukui Hyomemon Yoshihira (福井兵右衛門嘉平) in the early 1700s, and the

- *Hokushin Itto-ryu* (北辰一刀流), founded around the 1820's by Chiba Shusaku Narimasa (千葉 周作 成政, 1794 – 1856), who opened the popular *Chiba Dojo.*

A coalition of often-quarreling young swordsmen, the *Shinsengumi* practiced an amalgam of several styles, mostly based on the *Itto-ryu* ("One Sword" style) of Ito Ittosai Kagehisa (1550-1653?). Members of the *Shinsengumi* came from several of these styles, and likely quite a few others.

Sakurai Gennoshin Fumitaka, who would have been in his early or middle teens at the time of the Shinsengumi, was a follower of Kotaka's great-grand-uncle, Harada Sanosuke (原田 左之助, 1840-1868), the captain of the 10th Unit of the Shinsengumi. Harada supposedly had studied *Tyokushin-ryu Kenjutsu*, an obscure style, but was also a master of the famous *Hozoin-ryu* (宝蔵院流) spearmanship. Harada fought at the Battle of Ueno on July 4, 1868, where he was severely wounded by enemy gunfire. Two days later, he died of his wounds.*

According to an interview with Dr. Kotaka in the late 1990s, Sakurai Gen'noshin was the youngest first-cousin of Kotaka's great-grandfather, Kotaka Uranosuke Yoshisada. Sakurai learned *Kogen Itto-ryu* from Kotaka's great-great-grandfather (probably named Kotaka Shinsaemon Hidemichi, a *menkyo kaiden* in *Kogen Itto-ryu*) and his great-grandfather.

---

* There was a rumor that Harada did not die in 1868, however, but survived and travelled to China and became a leader for a group of horse-riding bandits. There were reports that an old Japanese man came to the aid of the Imperial Japanese Army in the First Sino-Japanese War—1894-1895—and claimed to be Harada Sanosuke. This was reported in a newspaper in 1965, but remains unsubstantiated and is unlikely.

Martial Arts, Styles, & Rankings of the Main Shinsengumi Members*

Name	Position	Style	Rank
Kondo Isamu	Commander	*Tennen Rishin-ryu*	*Menkyo kaiden*
Serizawa Kamo	Commander	*Shinto Munen-ryu*	*Menkyo kaiden*
Niimi Nishiki	Commander	*Shinto Munen-ryu*	*Menkyo kaiden*
Yamanami Keisuke	Vice commander/General Secretary	*Hokushin Itto-ryu*	*Menkyo kaiden*
Hijikata Toshizo	Vice commander	*Tennen Rishin-ryu*	*Mokuroku*
Ito Kashitaro	Staff Officer/ Military Advisor	*Shinto Munen-ryu* & *Hokushin Itto-ryu*	*Menkyo kaiden*
Okita Soji	Capt. 1st Unit	*Tennen Rishin-ryu*	*Menkyo kaiden*
Nagakura Shinpachi	Capt. 2nd Unit	*Shinto Munen-ryu*	*Menkyo kaiden*
Saito Hajime	Capt. 3rd Unit	*Mugai-ryu?*	n/a ("Master")
Matsubara Chuji	Capt. 4th Unit	*Sekiguchi-ryu Jujutsu*	n/a ("Master")
Takeda Kanryusai	Capt. 5th Unit	*Hokushin Itto-ryu/ Koshu Ryu Gungaku* ♦	n/a
Inoue Genzaburo	Capt. 6th Unit	*Tennen Rishin-ryu*	*Menkyo*
Tani Sanjuro	Capt. 7th Unit	*Jikishin-ryu* and *Shin-kage-ryu? Tyokushin Ryu . Taneda Houzou-in-ryu Sojutsu*	*Menkyo kaiden* in *Sojutsu* (spear).
Todo Heisuke	Capt. 8th Unit	*Hokushin Itto-ryu*	*Mokuroku*
Suzuki Mikisaburo	Capt. 9th Unit	*Shinto Munen-ryu*	n/a
Harada Sanosuke	Capt. 10th Unit	*Taneda Houzou-in-ryu Sojutsu*	*Menkyo kaiden*

Continued on next page

* At various times. Some of these individuals died, were killed, committed *seppuku*, were captured, or disappeared. See Appendix F for comments on ranks.
♦ ‾ Mainly a strategic advisor not a swordsman.

Martial Arts, Styles, & Rankings of the Main Shinsengumi Members (Continued)

Name	Position	Style	Rank
Hirayama Goro	Original member of *Roshigumi*	*Shinto Munen-ryu*	*Menkyo kaiden*
Noguchi Kenji	"	*Shinto Munen-ryu*	*Mokuroku*
Hirama Jusuke	"	*Shinto Munen-ryu*	*Mokuroku*
Ogata Shintaro	n/a	n/a	Scholar
Yamazaki Susumu	Inspector (external & internal spy)	*Kadori-ryu Bojutsu*	n/a. Doctor.
Tani Mantaro	Younger brother of Tani Sanjuro	*Jikishin-ryu* and *Shin-kage Ryu. Tyokushin Ryu.?*	n/a (Operated a *kenjutsu dojo*)

The Shinsengumi Banner.

150

What about Sakurai? Two questions arise from these assertions: Is there any evidence that Sakurai Gennoshin Fumitaka was a member of the Shinsengumi? And could he really have been a member at such a young age?

Sakurais in the Shinsengumi. The answer to the first question is, possibly yes, but I have found no evidence of a person of the same name as Dr. Kotaka's instructor. An extensive list (in English) of the leaders and "regimental soldiers" of the Corps includes both "Sakurai Kazuma" and "Sakurai Yuunoshin" [*sic*]. (See Appendix C, pages 165-172.) Given the Japanese propensity to adopt new names at different stages of life, and to have multiple parts of their name, it is possible that one of these people is Dr. Kotaka's later teacher. Another intriguing clue is that Ito Kashitaro (伊東甲子太郎武明, 1835-1867), the military advisor to the Shinsengumi, a *menkyo kaiden* in *Hokushin Itto-ryu,* and a scholar in both Asian and western learning, lived for a time with a certain "Sakurai Shiorusaemon" (or Shirozaemon), who may have been related to the same family.[16]

Youngsters in the Shinsengumi. The answer, however, more likely lies in an answer to the second question. It was not unheard of for youngsters to join military service—in Japan or elsewhere. Only a few years before the Shinsengumi period, for example, Johnny Clem (August 13, 1851–May 13, 1937), a 10-year-old, joined the Union Army as a drummer during the U.S. Civil War. (He later rose to the rank of major general.)

Moreover, there were other very young members of the Shinsengumi. Kondo Shuhei (近藤周平, also known as Tani Masatake, 谷周平) was 15 when he joined his adoptive father, Kondo Isamu, in the Shinsengumi in 1863. Ichimura Tetsunosuke (市村鉄之助) was about 13 when he joined the Shinsengumi with his older brother Ichimura Tatsunosuke in 1867. He served as an attendant or page to Vice Commander Hijikata Toshizo. Finally, Inoue Taisuke (井上泰助) was the nephew of the Shinsengumi's 6th unit commander, Inoue Genzaburo (井上源三郎, 1829-1868). He was only ten years old when he joined in 1867 and served as Kondo Isamu's page.[17] Thus, it is quite possible that Sakurai was not an actual "member" of the Shinsengumi, but served as a teen-aged page, attendant, or "squire" to an older member of his family who was a member or to Harada Sanosuke (原田 左之助, 1840-1868), the commander of the Shinsengumi's 10th unit, the company of which Sakurai Gennoshin allegedly was a member.

In 1999, Kotaka clarified the background and training of Sakurai Gennoshin:

Sakurai *Sensei* learned *Kogen Itto-ryu kendo* from one of my ancestors, Kotaka Jinzaemon Toshimichi who was one of *Kogen Itto-ryu Soke Senseis*. [*Sic.*] Sakurai *Sensei* incorporated many *kendo* techniques and concepts acquired from his real sword fight experience and intensive *kendo* training at the Shinsen-gumi Dojo. He practiced with some of the best *kenkaku* that ever lived such as Kondo Isamu (our family pronounces Isamu instead of Isami as in novels, movies, etc.), Hijikata Toshizo, Okita Soji, Harada Sanosuke, Saito Hajime, et al...

All documents [about Sakurai and his training], if any ever existed, were burned by air raids and/or intentionally by fleeing swordsmen, including Sakurai *Sensei*. Sakurai *Sensei* was hunted down as a war criminal in both the post Meiji-ishin [Meiji Restoration] civil war as a member of the Shinsen-gumi and the post Pacific War Era as an extreme nationalist educator who advocated and euphemized [*sic.*] the war against Allies. Sakurai *Sensei* was captured, tried, and purged from keeping public offices and government jobs. Eventually, Emperor Meiji and General McArthur pardoned him, respectively.

With or without the pardons, Sakurai *Sensei* kept teaching *Kogen Itto-ryu*-based *kendo*, *samurai* ethics, classical Chinese and Japanese literature, and Japanese history emphasizing the rise and fall and the resurrection of the Genji Clans using above-ground or underground *dojo*s and schools. Most of the students were Genji Clansmen, in other words, my relatives. I was one of three youngest students. [18]

Conclusion. After the Meiji Restoration, both Sakurai and Kotaka Yoshisada (Kotaka Sadao's great-grandfather) became *kendo* instructors for the Hachioji Police Force. (Hachioji is one of the 23 wards, or districts, of Tokyo.)

Thus, it is clear that Kotaka Sadao and his teachers had an intimate historical relationship with the *Kogen Itto-ryu* still taught in Japan, although the styles had diverged widely over the years. Sakurai Gennoshin Fumitaka undoubtedly combined what he had learned of the *Hiruma-ha Kogen Itto-ryu* with what he picked up from the Shinsengumi masters of *Tennen Rishin-ryu, Shinto Munen-ryu,* and *Hokushin Itto-ryu,* as well as other styles. It is no surprise, therefore, that what Sakurai taught Kotaka Sadao some 50 or more years later did not look like the *Henmi-ha Kogen Itto-ryu.*

In his later years, Dr. Kotaka took to calling his style the *"Sakurai-ha Kaigen* [or *Kaigenji] Itto-ryu,"* possibly partly to distinguish it from the Henmi family's art. Perhaps he spoke most clearly in a 1999 comment that "I learned the Shinsengumi style *Itto-ryu."* Elsewhere, he told an interviewer, "I was fortunate to learn many variations of *Kohgen Itto-Ryu* as developed by the leaders of the Shinsen Gumi. While my own teacher, Sakurai *Sensei* specialized in the techniques for arresting Ronin, Okita Soshi [Soji], the youngest of the Shinsen Gumi Commanders, who suffered from tuberculosis, developed a method of *Kohgen Itto Ryu** which while maintaining a strong offense, nonetheless conserved the maximum amount of energy during a fight."

His art certainly was not the same as the current *Kogen Itto-ryu* of Japan, but had deep roots there and elsewhere.

甲源一刀流

Kogen Itto-ryu

---

* Note that Okita's main style was *Shinto Munnen-ryu.*

Appendix A

Kotaka Sadao's Published Scientific Papers

Overleaf: Kotaka Sadao in retirement in Florida, around 2010.

Krueger, Albert P., Kotaka, Sadao, Andriese, Paul C., "Some observations on the physiological effects of gaseous ions," in *International Journal of Biometeorology* (1962) 6: 33-48 , March 01, 1962.

Albert P. Krueger, Sadao Kotaka, Paul C. Andriese, and with the technical assistance of Eddie J. Reed, "Studies on the Effects of Gaseous Ions on Plant Growth: I. The influence of positive and negative air ions on the growth of Avena sativa," in *Journal of General Physiology,* Volume 45, No. 5, May 1962.

Albert P. Krueger, Paul C. Andriese, Sadao Kotaka, "The biological mechanism of air ion action: The effect of $CO_2 +$ in inhaled air on the blood level of 5-hydroxytryptamine in mice," *International Journal of Biometeorology,* Vol. 7, no. 1, pp. 3-16, 1963.

Albert P. Krueger, Sadao Kotaka, Paul C. Andriese, and with the technical assistance of S.M Lamprecht and E.J. Reed, "A Study of the Mechanism of Air-Ion-Induced Growth Simulation in Hordeum Vulgaris," *International Journal of Biometeorology,* Vol. 7, no. 1, pp. 17-25, February 1, 1963.

A.P. Krueger, S. Kotaka, P.C. Andriese, "Gaseous-ion-induced Stimulation of Cytochrome c Biosynthesis," *Nature*, Vol. 200, No. 4907, pp. 707-708, 1963.

A. P. Krueger, S. Kotaka, P. C. Andriese, "Studies on air-ion-enhanced iron chlorosis I. Active and residual iron, " *International Journal of Biometeorology,* Vol. 8, no. 1, pp. 5-16, 1964.

A. P. Krueger, S. Kotaka, P. C. Andriese, "The effect of air containing $O2 -, O2 +, CO2 -$ and $CO2 +$ on the growth of seedlings of Hordeum Vulgaris," *International Journal of Biometeorology,* Vol. 8, no. 1, pp. 17-25, 1964.

Sadao Kotaka, Albert P. Krueger, Paul C Andriese,"Effect of Air Ions on IAA Content of Barley Seedlings" *Plant and Cell Physiology*, 1965.

Krueger, Albert P.; Beckett, J. C.; Andriese, Paul C.; Kotaka, Sadao, "Studies on the Effects of Gaseous Ions on Plant Growth," in *The Journal of General Physiology*, Volume 45 (5): 897 – May 1, 1962.

Sadao Kotaka, from the Institute of Plant Biochemistry, Faculty of Science, the Tokyo University of Education, Tokyo, Japan, "The L-Amino Acid Oxidase from Silkworm Eggs (Bombyx mori L.)", in *The Journal of General Physiology,* Vol. 46, 1963.

Krueger, Albert P., Andriese, Paul C., Kotaka, Sadao, "The biological mechanism of air ion action: The effect of CO_2+ in inhaled air on the blood level of 5-hydroxytryptamine in mice," in *International Journal of Biometeorology*, (1963) 7: 3-16 , February 01, 1963.

Kotaka, Sadao; Krueger, Albert P.; Andriese, Paul C.; et al., "Air Ion Effects on the Oxygen Consumption of Barley Seedlings," *Nature* 208 (1965), S. 1112-1113.

A. P. Krueger, S. Kotaka, P. C. Andriese, "The effect of abnormally low concentrations of air ions on the growth of Hordeum vulgaris," *International Journal of Biometeorology*, Vol. 9, no. 3, pp. 201-209, 1965.

A. P. Krueger, P. C. Andriese, S. Kotaka, "The effects of inhaling non -ionized or positively ionized air containing 2–4% $CO2$ on the blood levels of 5-hydroxytryptamine in mice," *International Journal of Biometeorology*, Volume 10, Issue 1, pp 17-28, July 1966.

A. P. Krueger, S. Kotaka, K. Nishizawa, Y. Kogure, M. Takenobu, P. C. Andriese, "Air ion effects on the growth of the silkworm (BOMBYX MORi L.)," *International Journal of Biometeorology*, Vol. 10, no. 1, pp. 29-38, 1966.

S. Kotaka, A. P. Krueger, P. C. Andriese, "The effect of air ions on light-induced swelling and dark-induced shrinking of isolated chloroplasts," *International Journal of Biometeorology*, Vol. 12, no. 2, pp. 85-92, 1968.

A. P. Krueger, P. C. Andriese, S. Kotaka, "Small air ions: Their effect on blood levels of serotonin in terms of modern physical theory," *International Journal of Biometeorology*, Vol. 12, no. 3, pp. 225-239, 1968.

S. Kotaka, A. P. Krueger, "Air ion effects on EDTA-induced bleaching in green barley leaves," *International Journal of Biometeorology*, Vol. 12, no. 4, pp. 331-342, 1968.

Kotaka S, Krueger AP. "Some observations on the bleaching of ethylenediaminetetraacetic acid on green barley leaves." *Plant Physiology*, June 1969, Vol. 44(6):809–815.

Krueger, A. and Kotaka, S., "The Effects of Air Ions on Brain Levels of Serotonin in Mice", *International Journal of Biometeorology*, Vol. 13, No. 1, 1969, pp. 25-3 8.

A. P. Krueger, S. Kotaka, E. J. Reed, S. Turner, "The effect of air ions on bacterial and viral pneumonia in mice," *International Journal of Biometeorology,* Vol. 14, no. 3, pp. 247-260, 1970.

A. P. Krueger, S. Kotaka, E. J. Reed, "The course of experimental influenza in mice maintained in high concentrations of small negative air ions," *International Journal of Biometeorology*, Vol. 15, no. 1, pp. 5-10, 1971.

S. Kotaka, A. P. Krueger, "Air ion effects on RNAse activity in green barley leaves," *Journal: International Journal of Biometeorology,* Vol. 16, no. 1, pp. 1-11, 1972.

Kotaka, Sadao, "Effects of Air Ions on Microorganisms and Other Biological Materials", *CRC Critical Reviews in Microbiology,* Nov 1978, pp. 109-149.

Appendix B

David Diguangco's
Curriculum Vitae

 # BIOGRAPHY
UNITED
STATES AIR
FORCE

David A. Diguangco

EDUCATION

BS Business Administration, Transportation and Logistics, double major Marketing, minor Statistics
The Ohio State University, Columbus, Ohio 1985

Specialized training:
Level II Acquisition Program Management Certificate, Defense Acquisition University, 2008
Certificates, Air Force Institute of Technology, Wright Patterson AFB, OH 1986 - 2004
U.S. Naval School, Explosive Ordnance Disposal, VIP course, Indianhead, MD, 1995
F-16 Fighter Aircraft Familiarization Course, Hill AFB, UT 1992
Production Management Internship, Sikorsky Helicopters, Stratford, Connecticut, 1989
Supply Officer School, Lowry AFB, Denver, CO 1987

ASSIGNMENTS

Section Chief, Ground Mechanical, ICBM Ground Systems Division, 2013 – Present
Acquisition Program Manager, Ground Systems, ICBM Cryptography Upgrade, 2008 – 2013
Acquisition Program Manager, Ground Systems, ICBM Remote Visual Assessment, 2007 – 2008
Acquisition Program Manager, Ground Systems, ICBM Cryptography Upgrade, 2004 – 2007
Program Manager, ICBM Systems Engineering, Parts, Materials and Processes, 2002 - 2004
Program Manager, F-16 Fighter Aircraft Radar Program, 2001 - 2002
Program Manager, Mission Planning, Space & C3I Directorate, 1999 – 2001
Item Manager, Munitions and Explosives Ordnance Disposal, 1994 – 1999
Contracting Officer, Commodities, 1996

Project Administration Officer, F-16 Fighter Aircraft Directorate, 1994 - 1995
Modification Manager, F-16 Fighter Aircraft Directorate, 1991 – 1994
Production Manager, F-16 Fighter Aircraft Directorate, 1989 – 1991
Item Manager, (PALACE ACQUIRE), Training Devices Directorate, 1985 -1989

MAJOR AWARDS AND DECORATIONS

Certificate of Recognition, Engineering and Technical Support, ICBM Unauthorized Launch, 2011
Brent Scowcroft Award, ICBM SIV Team, 2005
Certificate of Appreciation, Mission Planning, Space & C3I Directorate, 2001
Certificate of Achievement, Munitions Directorate, 1999
Performance Award, Commodities Directorate, 1997
Explosives Ordnance Disposal Recognition Certificate, Air Force Materiel Command, 1994
Performance Award, Commodities Directorate, 1994
Notable Achievement Award, F-16 Fighter Aircraft Directorate, 1991
Certificate of Appreciation, Materiel Management Directorate, 1989
Performance Award, Materiel Management Directorate, 1988
Notable Achievement Award, Training Devices Directorate, 1985

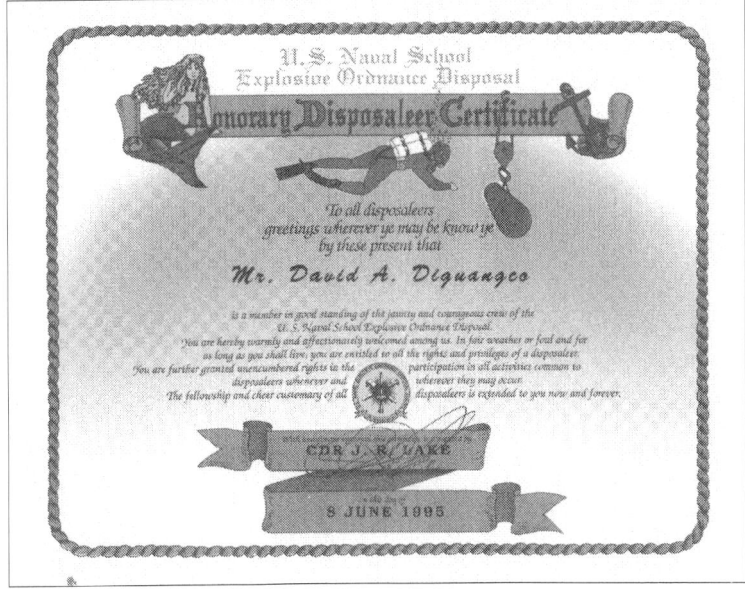

Appendix C

Shinsengumi's
Leaders & Members

Overleaf: Nagakura Shimpachi (永倉 新八), captain of the 2nd company of the Shinsengumi.

The original 13 members of the *Roshigumi* who founded the *Shinsengumi*:

Serizawa Kamo
Kondou Isamu
Hijikata Toshizo
Harada Sanosuke
Toudou Heisuke
Noguchi Kenji
Niimi Nishiki
Yamanami Keisuke
Okita Soji
Inoue Genzaburo
Hirayama Goro
Hirama Juusuke
Nagakura Shinpachi

Alleged original 24 members of the *Roshigumi* who founded the *Shinsengumi*:

Serizawa Kamo
Niimi Nishiki
Kondo Isamu
Negishi Yuuzan
Yamanami Keisuke
Saeki Matasaburo
Hijikata Toshizo
Okita Soji
Inoue Genzaburo
Hirayama Goro
Noguchi Kenji
Hirama Juusuke
Nagakura Shinpachi
Saito Hajime
Harada Sanosuke
Todo Heisuke
Iesato Jiro
Endo Jouan
Tonouchi Yoshio
Plus Kasuya Shingoro, Ueshiro Junnosuke, Suzuki Nagakura, Abira Eisaburo, who didn't report for duty due to illness.

Mibu *Roshigumi*
壬生 浪士組

Serizawa Kamo (Commander)
Niimi Nishiki (Commander, later Vice commander)
Abiru Eisaburo
Endo Joan
Hirama Jusuke
Hirayama Goro
Iesato Jiro
Kamishiro Jinnosuke
Kasuya Shingoro
Negishi Yuzan
Noguchi Kenji
Saeki Matasaburo
Shimizu Goichi
Suzuki Chozo
Tonouchi Yoshio

Officers of the *Shinsengumi* (1865)

Commander (局長, *Kyokucho*)
Kondo Isamu

Vice Commander (副長, *Fuku-cho*)
Hijikata Toshizo

General Secretary (総長, *Socho*)
Yamanami Keisuke

Staff Officer (参謀, *Sanbo*)
Ito Kashitaro

Captains (組長, *Kumicho*)
Okita Soji (1st Unit)
Nagakura Shinpachi (2nd Unit)
Saito Hajime (3rd Unit & commander in the Battle of Aizu)
Matsubara Chuji (4th Unit)

Takeda Kanryusai (5th Unit)
Inoue Genzaburo (6th Unit)
Tani Sanjuro (7th Unit)
Todo Heisuke (8th Unit)
Suzuki Mikisaburo (9th Unit)
Harada Sanosuke (10th Unit)

Spies/Investigators (監察方,
 Kansatsugata)
Yamazaki Susumu
Asano Kaoru
Shinohara Tainoshin
Arai Tadao
Hattori Takeo
Ashiya Noboru
Yoshimura Kanichiro
Ogata Shuntaro (later captain)
Oishi Kuwajiro
Yasutomi Saisuke (later vice
 commander)

"Corporals" (伍長, *Gocho*)
Abe Juro
Hashimoto Kaisuke
Hayashi Shintaro
Ibaraki Tsukasa
Ikeda Kotaro
Ito Tetsugoro
Kano Washio
Kawashima Katsuji
Kazurayama Takehachiro
Kondo Yoshisuke
Kumebe Masachika
Maeno Goro
Nakamura Kosaburo
Nakanishi Noboru
Obara Kozo
Okuzawa Eisuke
Ozeki Masajiro
Shimada Kai
Tomiyama Yahei

Accountants (勘定方,
 Kanjo-gata)
Kawai Kisaburo

Ozeki Yashiro
Sakai Hyogo
Kishijima Yoshitaro

Other Members
(At various times. Altogether
there were more than 400.)

1. Aiba Kunzaburo
2. Aoki Ren
3. Aoyama Jiro
4. Akashi Kakushiro
5. Akiyama Gisaburo
6. Adachi Rintaro
7. Abe Junta
8. Amaji Issen
9. Amami Katsunoshin
10. Aya Ichiro
11. Arai Hamao
12. Araki Shintaro
13. Arakida Samanosuke
14. Aridoshi Kango
15. Aridoshi Shimenoshin
16. Ieki Shougen
17. Igarashi Iori
18. Igi Hachiro
19. Ikeda Shichisaburo
20. Ikeda Shouji
21. Ishii Inosuke
22. Ishii Yujiro
23. Ishikawa Saburo
24. Ishida Nyugo
25. Ichinose Kanji
26. Ichihashi Kamakichi
27. Ichimura Tatsunosuke
28. Ichimura Tetsunosuke
29. Isshiki Zennojo
30. Itsumi Katsusaburo
31. Ito Kazue
32. Ito Naminosuke
33. Ito Hayanosuke
34. Ito Yahachirou
35. Inayoshi Yuzaburo
36. Inoue Genzaemon

37.Inoue Taisuke
38.Iwasaki Ichiro
39.Iwasaki Katsujiro
40.Ingu Umasaku
41.Uesaka Koutaro
42.Ueda Adachinosuke
43.Ueda Umanojo
44.Ueda Kingo
45.Ueda Matsuji
46.Uehara Eisaku
47.Ueyama Eihachi
48.Uchiyama Motojiro
49.Utsumi Jiro
50.Umedo Katsunoshin
51.Egawa Shichiro
52.Echigo Saburo
53.Ebata Kotaro
54.Ouchi Yarinosuke
55.Otani Yoshisuke
56.Otsuki Touzo
57.Ono Uchu
58.Oono Kuranosuke
59.Ohashi Hanzaburo
60.Ohashi Yamasaburo
61.Omachi Tsunataro
62.Omura Ataka
63.Okada Katsumi
64.Okada Goro
65.Okada Yonetaro
66.Okado Manjiro
67.Okamura Kametaro
68.Ogawa Issaku
69.Ogawa Shintaro
70.Okita Shounoshin
71.Ozawa Soji
72.Obata Saburo
73.Ohara Kinzo
74.Kagatsume Katsunoshin
75.Kajitani Rinnosuke
76.Kasuya Kojiro
77.Kasuya Juro
78.Kato Kumagoro
79.Kato Sadakichi
80.Kato Tamiya
81.Kato Higuma

82.Kadogaya Tadasu
83.Kaneko Shoubee
84.Kaneko Jirosaku
85.Kamei Mikinosuke
86.Karashima Shouji
87.Kawai Tetsugoro
88.Kawai Yasaburo
89.Kawai Heizo
90.Kawamura Yazoemon
91.Kawamura Rinjiro
92.Kanabe Shiro
93.Kiuchi Mineta
94.Kikuchi Ou
95.Kishida Kenkichi
96.Kinoshita Katsuzo
97.Kihata Katsunoshin
98.Kihata Saburo
99.Kimura Katsunosuke
100.Kimura Chujiro
101.Kimura Hirota
102.Kimura Yoshinosuke
103.Kiyohara Kiyoshi
104.Kusakabe Shiro
105.Kusakabe Toomi
106.Kusunoki Kojuro
107.Kumazawa Motozo
108.Kurihara Sennosuke
109.Kurokawa Sakichi
110.Kokubo Seikichi
111.Koshinoumi
112.Kojima Mikinojo
113.Goto Daisuke
114.Kobayashi Keinosuke
115.Kobayashi Koujiro
116.Kobayashi Minetaro
117.Kobari Seiichiro
118.Saito Shuuzen
119.Saito Seiichirou (some say Ichidakusai?)
120.Sakai Youjiro
121.Sakamoto Heizo
122.Sakuma Gintaro
123.Sakuma Kensuke
124.Sakuma Soutaro
125.Sakuma Norito

126.Sakurai Kazuma
127.Sakurai Yuunoshin
128.Sasaki Aijiro
129.Sasaki Kuranosuke
130.Sasaki Hajime
131.Sasazuka Minezo
132.Sashida Takejiro
133.Saji Hiroshi
134.Sato Fusataro
135.Sano Shimenosuke
136.Sano Makita
137.Sawa Chuusuke
138.Shiosawa Rinjiro
139.Shikauchi Chikara
140.Shinozaki Shinbachiro
141.Shibaoka Mansuke
142.Shibata Hikosaburo
143.Shibayama Tokusaburo
144.Shiba Ryousaku
145.Shiba Rokunosuke
146.Shibusawa Kichinosuke
147.Shimada Konosuke
148.Shimada Yaichiro
149.Shimizu Ukichi
150.Shimizu Kyuzaemon
151.Shukuin Ryuzo
152.Shouji Heizaburo
153.Shirai Takanoshin
154.Shirato Tomoe
155.Shirahara Shichirouemon
156.Sugano Rokuro
157.Sugiyama Youji
158.Suzuki Naoto
159.Suzuki Ryohei
160.Suzuki Renzaburo
161.Suwa Ichijiro
162.Sekikawa Daijiro
163.Sekikuchi Fusataro
164.Seyama Takito
165.Senda Hyoue
166.Souma Kazue
167.Daimatsu Keisai
168.Tauchi Tomo
169.Taoka Taro
170.Takaoka Kurataro
171.Takasu Kumao
172.Takada Bunjiro
173.Takano Ryouemon
174.Takahashi Kyousuke
175.Takahashi Wataru
176.Takayama Jiro
177.Takeuchi Gentaro
178.Takeuchi Tokuhei
179.Takeshiro Kurata
180.Takenouchi Takeo
181.Takenouchi Tokuo
182.Takebe Ginjiro
183.Tachikawa Chikara
184.Tagouro Hiroto
185.Tanaka Umetaro
186.Tanaka Torazo
187.Tanaka Ritsuzo
188.Tani Mantaro
189.Tanigawa Tatsukichi
190.Taniguchi Shirobee
191.Tamaoki Ryouzo
192.Tamgawa Masanosuke
193.Tamura Ichiro
194.Tamura Kinshichiro
195.Tamura Ginnosuke
196.Tamura Daizuburo
197.Tamura Rokushiro
198.Chiba Sakae
199.Tsukamoto Zennosuke
200.Tsuga Ushigoro
201.Tsuchida Shinnojo
202.Tsubota Chouzo
203.Tsuruoka Kenshiro
204.Terai Chikara
205.Terashima Hanzou
206.Toba Takimatsu
207.Tomigawa Juro
208.Tominaga Masanosuke
209.Nakai Mitsuya
210.Nakagawa Kojuro
211.Nakazawa Tsutomu
212.Nogasawa Masanojo
213.Nagashima Gorosaku
214.Nakajima Nobori
215.Nakajio Tsunehachiro

216.Nagase Seizo
217.Nagata Kamasaburo
218.Nakamura Kichiroku
219.Nakamura Kyuma
220.Nakamura Kingo
221.Nakamura Koro
222.Nakamura Seishichi
223.Nakayama Juzo
224.Nariai Kiyoshi
225.Nishizawa Yoshikichi
226.Nishimura Isogoro
227.Nishimura Kozaemon
228.Nishimura Kanzaburo
229.Nishimura Genrokuro
230.Nitta Kakuzaemon
231.Nitta Toranosuke
232.Numajiri Aijiro
233.Nobu Tamio
234.Nomura Yuuki
235.Nomura Risaburo
236.Hatakeyama Yoshijiro
237.Hamaguchi Hiichi
238.Hayashi Kyukichi
239.Hayashi Kogoro
240.Hayashi Shoukichi
241.Hayashi Takenosuke
242.Hijikata Tsushima
243.Fukuda Katsunoshin
244.Fukuyo Onari
245.Fujii Yasuhachi
246.Fujisawa Takeki
247.Fujimoto Kichinosuke
248.Fujimoto Hikonosuke
249.Fujiwara Wasaburo
250.Funazu Kamataro
251.Furukawa Kojiro
252.Furuya Jounosuke
253.Hoshikawa Sanbei
254.Hosoi Shikaranosuke
255.Hosokawa Sentaro
256.Hosokawa Takumi
257.Honda Iwakichi
258.Honda Taichiro
259.Maeda Iwataro
260.Maeda Kurando

261.Maeda Kijima
262.Maeda Kogoro
263.Makino Genshichiro
264.Magoshi Daitaro
265.Masaki Orinosuke
266.Mazaki Takutaro
267.Matsui Tokutaro
268.Matsui Ryuzaburo
269.Matsuzaki Shizumi
270.Matsuzawa Otozo
271.Matsuzawa Danji
272.Matsuda Rokuro
273.Matsunaga Kazue
274.Matsubara Ikutaro
275.Mazume Shinjuro
276.Matzume Ryutaro
277.Matsumoto Kijiro
278.Matsumoto Shuzo
279.Matsumoto Sutesuke
280.Matsumoto Chikara
281.Maruo Keijiro
282.Maruyama Konnosuke
283.Manda Kozo
284.Miura Keinosuke
285.Miura Shigetaro
286.Miura Tsunujiro
287.Miura Matsugoro
288.Miura Isetake
289.Mishina Ichiro
290.Mishina Jiro
291.Mishina Chuuji
292.Mizuguchi Ichimatsu
293.Mizutani Toshichi
294.Mitsui Ushinosuke
295.Miyagawa Kazumi
296.Miyagawa Nobukichi
297.Miyagaki Hannojo
298.Miyatake Orizo
299.Miyamoto Touta
300.Miyoshi Yutaka
301.Mukaidate Noboru
302.Muto Matasaburo
303.Murakami Saburo
304.Murakami Monjiro
305.Murayama Kenkichi

171

306. Muro Takunosuke
307. Motoi Waichiro
308. Mototake Gonbei
309. Mori Rokunosuke
310. Mori Gonjiro
311. Mori Takanosuke
312. Mori Tsunukichi
313. Morishita Heisaku
314. Mori Rokuro
315. Yagane Shigezo
316. Yaguchi Kenichiro
317. Yanagisawa Touma
318. Yanagida Sanjiro
319. Yabe Hyogo
320. Yama Toranosuke
321. Yamaura Tetsushiro
322. Yamagata Tokitaro
323. Yamagiwa Heizaburo
324. Yamaguji Bunjiro
325. Yamazaki Hachizo
326. Yamazaki Ringoro
327. Yamada Harutaka
328. Yamano Yasohachi
329. Yamamoto Jisoroku
330. Yuuki Umunosuke
331. Yokoyama Nabejiro
332. Yoshizawa Heizo
333. Yoshimura Jiro
334. Yoshimura Shintaro
335. Yoshimura Yoshitaro
336. Wakada Eikichi
337. Wada Juro
338. Wada Hayato
339. Wada Rokuro
340. Wakada Kotouta
341. Wadaka Toranosuke
342. Watanabe Ichizo
343. Wado Teizo

Suzuki Mikisaburo, Captain of 9th Unit.

This is the only extant photo believed to be of Saito Hajime, Captain of the 3rd Unit and commander at the Battle of Aizu.

Sources: "Shinsengumi" at http://en.wikipedia.org/wiki/Shinsengumi; "Shinsengumi" ay http://wiki.samurai-archives.com/index.php?title=Shinsengumi; and http://hajimenokizu.com.

Appendix D

The Shinsengumi Code of Conduct

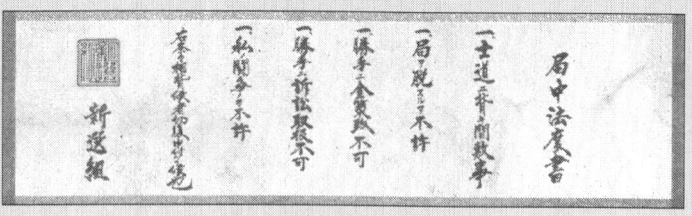

局中法度書

一　士道ニ背キ間敷事

一　局ヲ脱スルヲ不許

一　勝手ニ金策致不可

一　勝手ニ訴訟取扱不可

一　私ノ闘争ヲ不許

右条々相背候者切腹申付ベク候也

新選組

Overleaf: Shinsengumi Code of Conduct on scroll. Simulated act of *seppuku*, with *kaishaku* (assistant) poised to deliver the *coup de grace.*

The Shinsengumi established and enforced a very rigid and harsh Code of Conduct to keep its members in line and assure their loyalty. The Code mainly consisted of the following points, reportedly written by Vice Commander Hijikata Toshizo. Shinsengumi members were forbidden from:

- Deviating from Bushido.
- Leaving the Shinsengumi
- Raising money privately.
- Taking part in litigations.
- Engaging in private fights.
- Anybody who breaks the rules will be ordered to commit *seppuku.*

Other rules were also enforced, including:

- If the leader of a unit was mortally wounded in a fight, all the members of the unit must fight and die on the spot.
- Even in a fight where the death toll was high, the unit was not allowed to retrieve the bodies of the dead, except the corpse of the leader of the unit.
- If a Shinsengumi member engages in a fight with a stranger, be it on duty or not, if he is wounded and can't kill the enemy, allowing him to run away, even in case of a wound in the back, *seppuku* is ordered.

"Of the twenty-two most noted officers, only three survived those bloody times. At least six were assassinated, three committed *seppuku*, and two were executed. In 1876, eight years after the death of Kondo Isami and the final collapse of the Tokugawa Bakufu, in the Itabashi district of Tokyo—the new Eastern Capital—at a spot on the earth just a stone's throw from the execution grounds where Kondo had been beheaded, Nagakura erected a stone monument for the repose of the souls of his comrades who did not survive the revolution. Their names are engraved on the stone. Thirty-nine are listed as having died in battle, and seventy-one having met their end by disease, accident, *seppuku*, or execution."

Sources: "Shinsengumi" at http://en.wikipedia.org/wiki/Shinsengumi and Romulus Hillsborough, *Shinsengumi: The Shogun's Last Samurai Corps.* Rutland, VT: Tuttle, 2005 (quote from page 43).

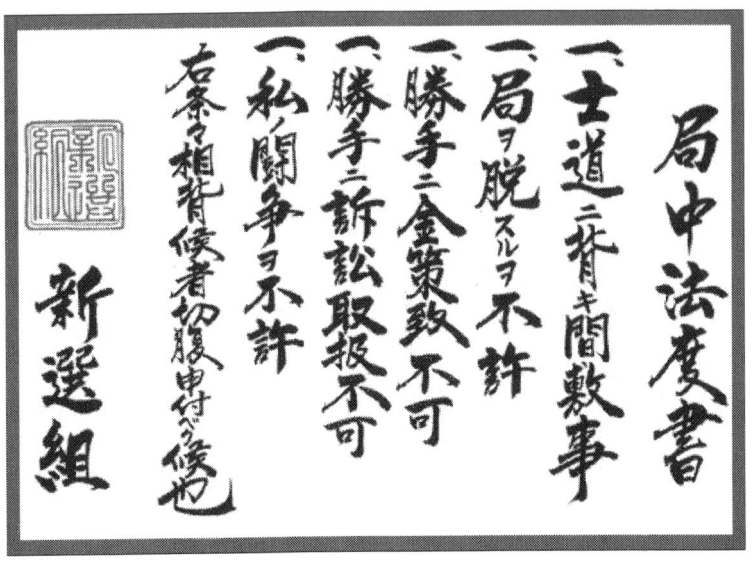

The Shinsengumi *"Gohatto,"* or Code of Conduct.

Appendix E

The Shinsengumi
Flag, Motto, and Uniform

Overleaf: Shinsengumi banner. Note the presence of the Shinsengumi banner design behind Kotaka Sadao in the photo on the title page, above.

The members of the Shinsengumi were highly visible in battle due to their distinctive uniforms. Following the orders of Commander Serizawa Kamo, the standard uniform consisted of the *haori* (jacket) and *hakama* (pleated pants-skirt) over a *kimono* (robe), with a white cord called a *tasuki* crossed over the chest and tied in the back. The function of the *tasuki* was to prevent the sleeves of the *kimono* from interfering with movement of the arms during battle. The Shinsengumi often wore a light chain mail suit beneath their robes and a light helmet made of iron, which protected them from other fighters. They also wore a head band on which was inscribed the word, *makoto* (誠 "sincerity"). The uniform was most easily identified by the *haori*, which was colored *asagi-iro* (浅葱色, a light blue). The *haori* sleeves were trimmed with the "white mountain stripes." This gave their members a distinctive uniform, quite different from the usual browns, blacks, and grays found in warrior clothing.

The Shinsengumi banner or flag was composed of a red background with the character *makoto* (誠) emblazoned on the middle in white. The bottom of the flag, like the *haori* sleeves was trimmed with the "white mountain stripes." The banner "was approximately five feet long, nearly four feet wide. The corpsmen carried their distinguishing banner and wore their distinguishing uniforms on their daily patrols of the city…'the men of the Shinsengumi tied their topknots into great clumps of hair. When they walked against the wind the bushy ends would flare out wider, evoking an even more imposing spectacle'."

Makoto, usually translated as "sincerity," has very different overtones than the word would suggest in English. In modern Japanese, it is often used to mean "truth" and is a common personal name, mostly for boys. (The *Yakuza*, or Japanese underworld, still uses it as "sincerity" in the way the Shinsengumi intended.) Rather than the English translation of freedom from deceit, hypocrisy, or duplicity or honesty, in Japanese it connotes earnestness, loyalty, integrity, and fidelity, the willingness to give all for what one believes in or has committed oneself to. It was one of the "Seven Virtues of *Bushido*": loyalty (忠義, *chuugi*); respect (礼, *rei*), honor (名誉, *meiyo*), benevolence (慈悲, *jiin*), valor (勇気, *yuu*), rectitude (義, *gi*), and "sincerity" (*makoto*). The different meanings of sincerity

Source: "Shinsengumi" at http://en.wikipedia.org/wiki/Shinsengumi; Romulus Hillsborough, Shinsengumi: The Shogun's Last Samurai Corps. Rutland, VT: Tuttle, 2005 (quote from page 34); and http://www.stockkanji. com/Martial+Arts/%3Cb%3ESeven+Virtues+of+Bushido%3C%25252Fb% 3E.htm.

(*makoto*) for westerners and Japanese is nicely summed up in the words of one guide for foreign business people:

> Sincerity to most Westerners means free from pretense or deceit; in other words, honest and truthful without reservations. But the typical Japanese, being *Makoto (mah-koe-toe)* means to properly discharge all of one's obligations so that everything will flow smoothly and harmony will be maintained. It also means being careful not to say or do anything that would cause loss of face. By extension, it further means that *mokoto* people will not be self-seeking; will not get excited or provoke others to excitement; will not reveal their innermost thoughts if they are negative; will not, in fact, do anything disruptive.

> This, obviously, does not necessarily include or require strict adherence to what Westerners like to call honesty and frankness, since harmony of a kind can be maintained indefinitely as long as both sides play according to the same rules. And the Japanese, just like the Westerners, tend to think and behave as if their rules were the ones being used.*

Interestingly, the character *makoto* (誠) on the Shinsengumi flag is very similar to the character 試 in *Shieikan* (試衛館), the name of the *Tennen Rishin-ryu dojo* of Kondo Isamu. When he became the leader of Shinsengumi, he had to choose a character for the flag. According to one account, he wanted to use *shi* (試) from *Shieikan* (試衛館), but chose *makoto* instead, apparently as the closest character with a strong *samurai* meaning as he could find.♦

---

* Boye Lafayette De Mente's Asian Business Codewords at http://www.apm-forum.com/columns/boye49.htm.
♦ http://thekyotoproject.org/english/the-shinsengumi/.

Manikins in Shinsengumi garb (http://en.wikipedia.org/wiki/Shinsengumi).

Appendix F

Traditional *Koryu* *Kenjutsu* Ranks

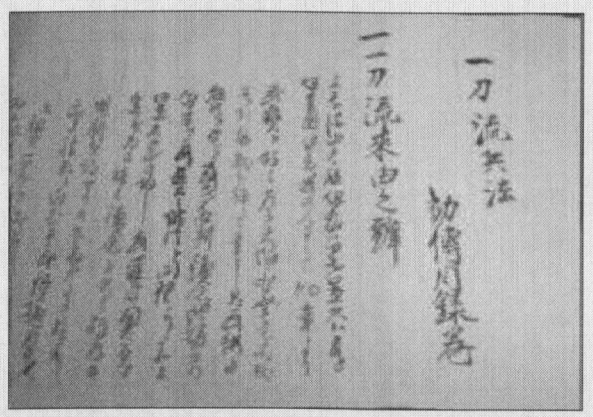

Overleaf: Photo of a portion of an *Itto-ryu Mokuroku*, or certification scroll.

Modern *kendo* has adopted the common *dan-kyu* grading system that is used in *judo*, *karate*, most other martial arts, and many other national arts in Japan, such as *ikebana* (flower arranging), *go* (a Sino-Japanese board game), and *shudo* (calligraphy). The old-style, pre-Meiji Restoration schools of martial arts—like those used by the members of the Shinsengumi—however, used different systems for denoting grade or rank. These varied from style to style and art to art.

According to one source, the *Tennen Rishin-ryu*, one of the major styles of swordsmanship in the Shinsengumi used: *Nyumon* (入門, Entering the gate; *Kirigami* (切紙, paper certificate, about 1.5 years from *Nyumon*); *Mokuroku* (目録, first scroll, about 1.5 years from *Kirigami*); *Chugokui Menkyo* (中極意, "mid-level license," 3+ years from *Mokuroku*); *Menkyo* (免許, license, about 4 years from *Chugokui Menkyo*); *Inka* (印可, "Seal," about 5 years from *Menkyo*); and *Shihan Menkyo* (師範免許, teacher's License, about 5 years from *Inka*). Another source lists only *Kirigami, Mokuroku, Chugokui Mokuroku,* and *Shihan Menkyo*.

According to one account, the *Shinto Munen-ryu* used only four gradings: *kirigami, murokuroku, jyu menkyo* (instructor certification), and *menkyo kaiden* (免許皆伝, full licensure). Some styles use as few as three grades, for example, *Okuiri* (奥入, "Entering the Secrets"), *Mokuroku* (目録), and *Menkyo* (免許). Others use *shoden* (初伝, first transmission), *chuden* (中伝, middle-level transmission), *joden* (上伝, upper-level transmission), *okuden* (奥伝, secret transmission), and *gokui* (極意, inner secrets).

As we have seen in the accounts of the Shinsengumi leaders, members, and even *kenjutsu* instructors, many people in their 20s, or even in their teens, held such relatively high ranks as *mokuroku, menkyo* and even *menkyo kaiden*. It is important to remember that these ranks were not really comparable to today's *dan-kyu* system. Today, relatively high rank takes a long time to achieve, curricula are often long and complicated, and seniority is very important.

At the time of the Shinsengumi, styles were generally much more compact, with some only including 10, 25, or 30 techniques. "Mastery" of these could be accomplished within a relatively few years. In the case of Okita Soji, for example, he entered the *dojo* at around age 10. By 12, he was recognized as a very promising student, even defeating a *kenjutsu* instructor from a neighboring *han* (prefecture). At 19, he was the head teacher of his *dojo* and a *menkyo kaiden*. Kondo Isamu was made headmaster of the entire *Tennen Rishin-ryu* at about the age of 27.

As well-known martial arts practitioner, author, and expert Ellis Amdur has noted, "I was shown a text [from the Meiji period] which had names of a number of people in three different *ryu* in Gumma [prefecture], with their start and finish dates. The average length of time from joining to *menkyo kaiden* was between 5-7 years. This was a time when Japan was actively expanding on the continent—a lot of war. I think young men had to toughen up and thus, in their teens, they joined, and were papered up by the time they went into the military. And given they were on their way to war, I bet they trained really hard, too."

He goes on to relate:

> I received *okuden menkyo* (the "highest" technical rank) in *Toda-ha Buko-ryu* in 1983. I joined in 1978. Nitta *sensei* skipped me over *chuden*.
>
> 1. I put in an insane number of hours of practice (Sawada *sensei* makes this point in her interview in Skoss' *Koryu Bujutsu*—that the number of years is not a good measure of how much practice one has actually done).
>
> 2. I continued to improve immeasurably after receiving *okuden*. The *menkyo* was a benchmark, not a "final" attainment.
>
> Similarly, one of my *Araki-ryu* students... is powerful in *judo/sambo* etc. There are 18 *kata* in the *torite* section of the *ryu*. I ranked him in this section in a period of six months. I showed it to him, he got it (and continues to practice it), but I have nothing more to teach him. He improves without any input, in a teaching sense, from me—in that section of the *ryu* at least. Why drag it out? If his, or any other students learning of the complete *ryu* happened equally fast, I'd make them *menkyo* and send them on their way. If they don't learn it, I'll never rank them.
>
> Taking "speed of rank" to an extreme, Kurokochi Dengoro, perhaps the strongest *bugeisha* in Aizu, during the late Edo, chased down a teacher of *Anazawa ryu naginatajutsu*. He had been forbidden to train with the man when he visited Aizu, so he went over the border into the next *han* and met with the man at an inn. Over a period of three days, he was taught the 36 *kata* of *Anazawa-ryu*, and given *menkyo kaiden*. He never saw his teacher again, and from that time forward, abandoned the *naginata ryu* he'd previously taught (among many other *ryu*) and taught *Anazawa-ryu*. *

---

* http://www.budoseek.net/vbulletin/archive/index.php/t-28157.html.

Sakurai-ha
Kogen Itto-ryu
Curriculum

Overleaf: Kotaka Sadao (right) engaging in *keiko* at the Covington, KY *karate dojo* of *Hanshi* William Dometrich, . Photo courtesy of Hisako Kotaka.

櫻井派甲源一刀流

Sakurai-ha Kogen Itto-ryu

興武館道場

Kobukan Dojo

第一部 基本稽古

Part 1. Basic Practice

一、準備運動	Junbi-undo	(Preparatory exercise)
二、構え	Kamae	(Stance)
1. 中段	Chudan	(Middle stance)
2. 上段	Jodan	(Upper stance)
3. 下段	Gedan	(Lower stance)
4. 八双	Hasso	
5. 脇構	Wakigamae	(Side stance)
6. 陽刀	Yoto	
7. 陰刀	Kage-to	
三、足捌	Ashisabaki	(Footwork)
1. 並足	Namiashi	
2. 継足	Tsugiashi	
基本竹刀稽古	Kihon shinai keiko	Basic shinai practice
素振り稽古	Suburi keiko	Swinging-in-air practice
（又は上稽古）	(or Uwageiko)	(Preparatory practice)
一、帯刀	Taito	Wear sword!
二、禮	Rei	Bow!
三、抜け刀	Nuke to	Draw sword!
四、前後面打ち	Zengo menuchi	Front and back men strike

189

五、前後左右面打ち	Zengo sayuu men uchi	Front/back/left/right men strike
用意	Yoi	Ready!
始め	Hajime	Go!
止め	Yame	Cease (whatever you are doing)!
六、篭手面胴	Kote/men/do	Continuous kote/men/do strikes
用意	Yoi	Ready!
始め	Hajime	Go!
篭手、面、胴	Kote, men, do	Move forward
一、二、三	Ichi, ni, san	Move backward
止め	Yame	Cease (whatever you are doing).
七、跳躍素振り	Choyaku suburi	Jumping suburi
用意	Yoi	Ready!
始め	Hajime	Go!
止め	Yame	Cease (whatever you are doing)!
八、飛び込み面	Tobikomi men	Dashing-in men
用意	Yoi	Ready!
始め	Hajime	Go!
止め	Yame	Cease (whatever you are doing)!
九、飛び込み篭手面	Tobikomi kote men	Dash-in kote men strikes
用意	Yoi	Ready!
始め	Hajime	Go!
止め	Yame	Cease (whatever you are doing)!
十、飛び込み篭手面胴	Tobikomi kote men do	Dash-in kote men do
用意	Yoi	Ready!
始め	Hajime	Go!
止め	Yame	Cease (whatever you are doing)!
十一、飛び込み篭手篭手面	Tobikomi kote kote men	Dash-in kote kote men

打ち込み稽古	Uchikomi keiko	Full-contact practice
一、斬り返し	Kirikaeshi	Repeating men cuts
二、面	Men	Dashing-in men strike
三、胴	Do	Dashing-in do strike
四、篭手・面・胴	Kote, men, do	Dashing-in kote, men, do strikes
五、掛稽古	Kakari geiko	Quick random strikes on any parts in any combinations
六、地稽古（稽古）	Jigeiko (Keiko)	Full-contact tournament-like practice

櫻井派甲斐源氏（甲源）一刀流基本型其の一

Sakurai-ha Kai-genji (Kogen) Itto-ryu Basic Kata 1

（新撰組/見廻組刀法）

(Shinsen-gumi/Mimawari-gumi Toho[Sword Techniaues])

大刀の部

Dai-to no Bu

一本目
First technique

入刃斬落面
Iri-ha Kiri-otoshi Men

二本目
Second technique

出刃斬落突
De-ha Kiri-otoshi Tsuki

三本目
Third technique

篭手陽刀抜外篭手返付込胴突斬
Kote Yoto Nuki-hazushi Kote-gaeshi
Tsuke-komi Do Tsuki-kiri

四本目
Fourth technique

撥篭手返付込胴突斬
Haji-kote-gaeshi Tsuke-gomi Do-tsuki-giri

五本目
Fifth technique

陽刀払捨右胴斬
Yo-to Hossha Migi-do-giri

六本目
Sixth technique

陰刀払捨左胴斬
Kage-to Hossha Hidari-do-giri

七本目

Seventh technique

篭手斬払捨右胴斬

Kote-giri Hossha Migi-do-giri

八本目

Eighth technique

篭手斬払捨左胴斬

Kote-giri Hossha Hidari-do-giri

九本目

Ninth technique

水車双手斬

Mizu-guruma Morote-giri
(Hidari Mizu-guruma)

十本目

Tenth technique

大車双手撫斬

O-guruma Morote Nade-giri

十一本目

Eleventh technique

飛竜剣

Hiryu Ken

十二本目

Twelfth technique

旋竜剣

Senyu Ken

櫻井派甲源一刀流
Sakurai-ha Kohgen Itto-ryu
鬼篭手大刀乃型
Oni-gote Daitoh no Kata

太刀配り
Tachi Kubari

一本目

Ippon-me

対大上段入刃切落

Iriha Kiriotoshi against Dai (Grand) Jyodan

二本目

Nihon-me

対大神楽上段入刃切落

Iriha Kiriotoshi against Dai (Grand) Kagura Jyodan

三本目

Sanbon-me

同影入刃切落

Doei Iriha Kiriotoshi

四本目

Yonhon-me

対大晴眼出刃切落

Deha Kiriotoshi against Dai Seigan

五本目

Gohon-me

対大晴眼出刃切落突斬り

Deha Kiriotoshi Tsuki-kiri against Dai Seigan

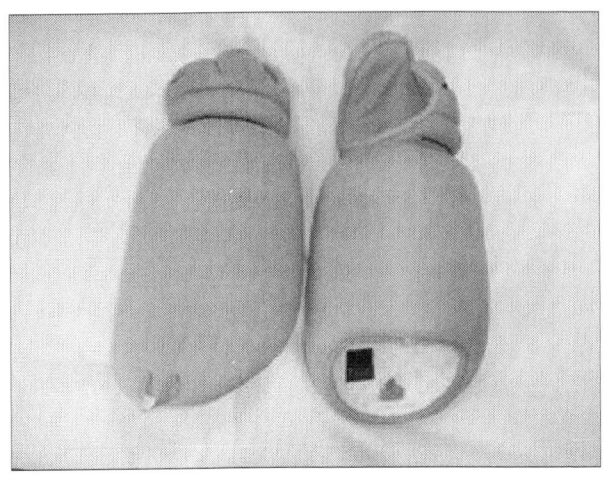

Oni gote

Yaginuma Sachiko demonstrating *Hokushin Itto-ryu* with her father, the famous Yaniguma Tessui (wearing *onigote*) around 1956. Tessui's three daughters were among the pioneering women in modern *kendo.* Setsuko was the
first All Japan Ladies Kendo Champion in May 1962. Later (under her mar-
ries name of Kobayashi Setsuko, she became the second person to pass the
test for 7th *dan* on the 8th of May 1991. Between 1955-1964,) Setsuko performed demonstrations of *Hokushin-Itto-Ryu* with Tessui at the Tomioka
Hachimangu Shrine. Tessui used a pair of Onigote he had made himself.

Notes

Notes to Part I

1. Interview conducted in 1998 by Phil Fellman, Ph.D. of *Hokushin Itto-ryu* and *Kameyama-ha Owari Yagyu-ryu* available on http://listserve.uoguelph.ca/cgi-bin/wa?a2=ind9810&L=iaido-l&D=0&F=P&P=5587, accessed September 16, 2009 and Jane Van Paepeghem, "'A Samurai Never Dies, Just Becomes A Hue of the Sword'," *Ohio Martial Artist*, Vol. 1, No. 11, August 1985.
2. *Ibid.*
3. *Ibid* and also Sadao Kotaka, Ph.D., "The Relativistic Quantization of a Classical Kendo," formerly posted on the website of the Classical Kendo Federation (no longer available); email message from Kotaka Sadao to "Japanese Sword Mailing List" dated May 25, 1999; and Kotaka Sukesaburo (Minamotono) Sadayasu [Sadao], "A legend of Sakurai-ha Kaigenji (Kogen) Itto-ryu" from Japanese Sword Art Mailing List, March 2, 2000.
4. The best study in English of the *Shinsengumi* is Romulus Hillsborough, *Shinsengumi: The Shogun's Last Samurai Corps.* Rutland, VT: Tuttle, 2005. See also Hillsborough, *Samurai Sketches From the Bloody Final Years of the Shogun.* San Francisco: Ridgeback Press, 2001; Hillsborough, *Ryoma: Life of a Renaissance Samurai.* San Francisco: Ridgeback Press, 1999; Hillsborough, *Samurai Tales: Courage, Fidelity, and Revenge in the Final Years of the Shogun.* Rutland, VT: Tuttle, 2010; Ryotaro Shiba, *The Last Shogun: The Life of Tokugawa Yoshinobu.* New York: Kodansha, 1988; Marius Jansen, *Sakamoto Ryoma and the Meiji Restoration.* New York: Columbia University Press, 1995; and Hillsborough, *Samurai Revolution: The Dawn of Modern Japan Seen Through the Eyes of the Shogun's Last Samurai.* Rutland, VT: Tuttle, 2014. On the general period, see especially Marius B. Jansen, *The Making of Modern Japan.* Cambridge, MA: Harvard University, 2000 and Donald Keene, *Emperor of Japan: Meiji and His World, 1852-1912.* New York: Columbia University Press, 2002.
5. David Diguangco interview with Kotaka Sadao reported in *The Iaido Newsletter,* Volume 7, Number 11 #63 November 1995, available at http://www.collectionscanada.gc.ca/eppp-archive/100/202/300/iaido/1995/tin63.html.
6. *Ibid.*
7. Handwritten paper in the private collection of the author.
8. Diguangco interview with Sadao Kotaka. This is according to Kotaka's own words. In view of his later graduate work, it is not clear if he was referring to Tokyo University ("*Todai*") or the Tokyo University of Education, at which he did his graduate work. See below.

9. Van Paepeghem, "'A Samurai Never Dies, Just Becomes A Hue of the Sword'."

10. Diguangco interview with Sadao Kotaka. See also Sadao Kotaka, "The L-Amino Acid Oxidase from Silkworm Eggs," *The Journal of General Physiology,* Volume 46, 1963 at http://europepmc.org/articles/PMC2195297/pdf/1087.pdf and "Final Report of Contract #3656 (06)," 1967, at http://www.dtic.mil/cgi-bin/GetTR Doc?AD=AD660028. According to one of his former students, Kotaka may also have worked for the U.S. Navy in California as a physicist for a time after moving to the US. Posting by A.J. Bryant on *Kendo World* forum, 2009. He also later served as a consultant for the Honda Motors company in Ohio.

11. Van Paepeghem, "'A Samurai Never Dies, Just Becomes A Hue of the Sword'" and Diguangco interview with Sadao Kotaka.

12. At the time I trained with him, I recall him claiming a *sandan* ranking in *judo*. He later apparently told others his rank was *yodan.*

13. Van Paepeghem and Diguangco interview.

14. *Ibid.*

15. *Ibid.* and several internet forum postings.

16. Donald Yehling Internet posting on *Kendo World Forum,* July 8, 2009 and interview conducted in 1998 by Phil Fellman, Ph.D. of *Hokushin Itto-ryu* and *Kameyama-ha Owari Yagyu-ryu* available on http://listserve.uoguelph.ca/cgi-bin/wa?A2=ind9810&L=iaido -l&D=0&F=P&P=5587, accessed September 16, 2009.

17. United States Classical Kendo Federation web site (http://www.internationalclassicalkendofederation.org), no longer active.

18. A.J. Bryant, forum posting, June 24, 2009.

19. *Orlando Sentinel*, August 3, 2013.

20. *Sensei* never explained the details of this curse to me, but in a March 1987 letter to his student and friend, Dr. Tom Sovik, he explained that a curse had been laid on both his father's Kotaka clan and his mother's Omata clan, apparently by jealous rivals because they were "successful *samurai* clans." He deeply believed this, saying "my oldest aunt of [my] father's side was a media [*sic.*, medium] who could communicate with the spirit of deceased person[s]. She found the curse on me and gave me some advise to cope with this." "Because of this, I decided to come to this country and became a naturalized citizen. I had not practiced *kendo/ iaido* since my junior year in the Tokyo University (1955) until 1965. For some reasons, I started to practice *kendo/iaido,* hoping that the curse did not reach the U.S.A." He believed that the curse was connected to his daughter's untimely death.

21. For more information on Japanese history and the Seiwa Genji, see the numerous sources cited in the bibliography.
22. "Minamoto clan" at http://en.wikipedia.org/wiki/Minamoto_clan. The Minamoto was one of four "noble" clans, descended from emperors. The others were the Taira (Heishi), Fujiwara, and Tachibana. The Taira became the principal rivals of the Minamoto and fought several bloody wars for supremacy. Under the Minamoto, there were 21 sub-clans: Daigo Genji (descended from 60th emperor Daigo); Go-Daigo Genji (descended from 96th emperor Go-Daigo); Go-Fukakusa Genji (descended from 89th emperor Go-Fukakusa); Go-Nijo Genji (descended from 94th emperor Go-Nijo); Go-Saga Genji (descended from 88th emperor Go-Saga); Go-Sanjo Genji (descended from 71st emperor Go-Sanjo); Go-Shirakawa Genji (descended from 77th emperor Go-Shirakawa); Juntoku Genji (descended from 84th emperor Juntoku); Kameyama Genji (descended from 90th emperor Kameyama); Kazan Genji (descended from 65th emperor Kazan); Koko Genji (descended from 58th emperor Koko); Murakami Genji (descended from 62nd emperor Murakami); Montoku Genji (descended from 55th emperor Montoku); Nimmyo Genji (descended from 54th emperor Nimmyo); Ogimachi Genji (descended from 106th emperor Ogimachi); Reizei Genji (descended from 63rd emperor Reizei); Saga Genji (descended from 52nd emperor Saga); Sanjo Genji (descended from 67th emperor Sanjo); Seiwa Genji (descended from 56th emperor Seiwa); Uda Genji (descended from 59th emperor Uda); and Yozei Genji(descended from 57th emperor Yozei). The Seiwa Genji, one of the oldest, had three sub-clans: the Kawachi Genji (or Genke), which descended from Minamoto Yorinobu (968-1048), from which the Hitachi, Ishikawa, and Kai Genji families developed. **It was from the Kai Genji that Kotaka Sadao claimed descent.** The Kawata Genji were famous for producing the first three Kamakura shoguns. The second was the Settsu Genji descended from Minamoto Yorimitsu (948-1021), Yorinobu's brother. From the Settsu came the Tada, Mino, and Shinano Genji families. The last—the Yamato Genji—descended from Minamoto Yorichika (b. 954), also a brother of Yorinobu and Yorimitsu. See George Sansom, *A History of Japan to 1334.* Stanford, CA: Stanford University Press, 1958, pages 234 ff; Stephen Turnbull, *The Samurai Sourcebook.* London: Arms & Armour Press, 1998; "Clans" at *The Samurai Archives Samurai Wiki,* http://wiki.samurai-archives.com/index.php?title=Category: Clans; "Japanese Clans" at http://en.wikipedia.org/wiki/ Japanese_clans; "Minamoto Clan" at http://en.wikipedia.org/ wiki/Minamoto_clan; "Kamakura Shogunate" at http://en.

wikipedia.org/wiki/Kamakura_shogunate; and "Seiwa Genji" at http://en.wikipedia.org/wiki/Seiwa_Genji/.

23. On the following figures see Sansom, *A History of Japan to 1334* and Turnbull, *The Samurai Sourcebook*.

24. For brief sketches of Yoshiie, see, for example, Turnbull, *The Samurai Sourcebook*, page 60 and Michael Sharpe, *Samurai Leaders From the Tenth to the Nineteenth Century*. New York: Metro Books, 2008, 97-99. See especially Sansom, *A History of Japan to 1334;* Hiroaki Sato, *Legends of the Samurai*. Woodstock, NY: The Overlook Press, 1995, pages 95-109; and Paul Varley, *Warriors of Japan As Portrayed in the War Tales*. Honolulu: University of Hawaii, 1994, *passim*.

25. For brief sketches of Yoritomo, see Turnbull, *The Samurai Sourcebook*, page 60 and Sharpe, *Samurai Leaders From the Tenth to the Nineteenth Century*, pages 94-96. See especially Sansom, *A History of Japan to 1334;* Varley, *Warriors of Japan As Portrayed in the War Tales;* William R. Wilson, (trans. and annotated.) *Hogen Monogatari: Tale of the Disorder in Hogen*. Tokyo: Sophia University,1971; and Donald Keene, *Seeds in the Heart: Japanese Literature from Earliest Times to the Late Sixteenth Century*. New York: Henry Holt, & Co., 1993, pages 616 ff.

26. The literature on Yoshitsune is huge. For brief sketches see Turnbull, *The Samurai Sourcebook*, page 60; Sharpe, *Samurai Leaders From the Tenth to the Nineteenth Century*, pages 108-111; Varley, *Warriors of Japan As Portrayed in the War Tales*; Helen Craig McCullough, (trans. and introduction). *Yoshitsune: A Fifteenth-Century Japanese Chronicle*. Stanford, CA: Stanford University, 1971; A.L. Sadler, (trans.) *The Ten Foot Square Hut and Tales of the Heike*. Rutland, VT: Tuttle, 1972; Eiji Yoshikawa, *The Heike Story*. Rutland, VT: Tuttle, 1956; Hiroaki Sato, *Legends of the Samurai*. Woodstock, NY: The Overlook Press, 1995, pages 110-156; Ivan Morris, *The Nobility of Failure: Tragic Heroes in the History of Japan*. New York: Farrar, Straus and Giroux, 1975; Helen Craig McCullough, *The Tale of the Heike*. Stanford: Stanford University Press, 1988; Helen Craig McCullough, *Genji and Heike. Selections from "The Tale of Genji" and "The Tale of the Heike"*. Stanford: Stanford University Press, 1994; and Keene, *Seeds in the Heart: Japanese Literature from Earliest Times to the Late Sixteenth Century*, pages 629 ff.

27. See Christopher M. Clarke, *Samurai, Scoundrels, and Saints: Stories from the Martial Arts* (Second edition). Huntingtown, MD: Clarke's Canyon Press, 2011, pages 71-77.

28. For brief sketches of Takauji, see Turnbull, *The Samurai Source-book*, page 31; Sharpe, *Samurai Leaders From the Tenth to the Nineteenth Century*, pages 25-26. See especially, Sansom, *A History of Japan to 1334* and Varley, *Warriors of Japan As Portrayed in the War Tales*. See also "Ashikaga Takauji, 1305-1358" at http://www.samurai-archives.com/takauji.html and "Ashikaga Takauji" at http://en.wikipedia.org/wiki/Ashikaga_Takauji.

29. For brief sketches of Kusunogi Masashige see Turnbull, *The Samurai Sourcebook*, page 53; Sharpe, *Samurai Leaders From the Tenth to the Nineteenth Century*, pages 85-89. See especially, Sansom, *A History of Japan to 1334;* Varley, *Warriors of Japan As Portrayed in the War Tales*; Sato, *Legends of the Samurai,* pages 157-187; and Keene, *Seeds in the Heart: Japanese Literature from Earliest Times to the Late Sixteenth Century* pages 874-881. See also Christopher M. Clarke, *Samurai, Scoundrels, and Saints: Stories from the Martial Arts*, pages 93-101.

30. Cited in "Ashikaga Takauji" at http://en.wikipedia.org/wiki/Ashikaga_Takauji.

31. For brief sketches of Takeda Shingen, see Turnbull, *The Samurai Sourcebook*, page 81; Sharpe, *Samurai Leaders From the Tenth to the Nineteenth Century*, pages 163-164. See especially See especially, Sansom, *A History of Japan, 1334-1615;* Sato, *Legends of the Samurai,* pages 204-231; Clarke, *Samurai, Scoundrels, and Saints: Stories from the Martial Arts* (Second edition), pages 157-163; Stephen Turnbull, *Samurai Warlords: The Book of the Daimyo*. London: Blandford Press, 1989; Stephen Turnbull, *Battles of the Samurai*. London: Arms and Armour Press, 1987; and "Takeda Shingen, 1521-1573" at http://www.samurai-archives.com/shingen.html. For an interesting book on strategy, tactics, and weaponry arts by one of Shingen's advisors, see Thomas Cleary, (trans. and annotator). *Secrets of the Japanese Art of Warfare From the School of Certain Victory*. Rutland, VT: Tuttle, 2012.

32. The literature on the founder of the Tokugawa shogunate is huge. For brief sketches of Ieyasu, see Turnbull, *The Samurai Source-book*, page 85; Sharpe, *Samurai Leaders From the Tenth to the Nineteenth Century*, pages 165-170. See especially, Sansom, *A History of Japan, 1334-1615;* Conrad Totman, *Tokugawa Ieyasu, Shogun: A Biography*. Torrence, CA: Heian International, 1983; Turnbull, *Samurai Warlords;* Stephen Turnbull, *Tokugawa Ieyasu*. New York: Osprey, 2012; and A.L. Sadler, *The Maker of Modern Japan: The Life of Tokugawa Ieyasu*. New York: Taylor & Francis, 1937/2010. The sources of the art on the previous pages is as follows: Seiwa from http://en.wikipedia.org/wiki/

Emperor_Seiwa; Yoshiie from author's electronic collection; Yoritomo from http://en.wikipedia.org/wiki/Minamoto_no_Yoritomo; Yoshitoshi from http://en.wikipedia.org/wiki/File:Shingen by Utagawa Kuniyoshi (1798-1861) at http://en.wikipedia.org/wiki/Takeda_Shingen; Yoshitsune_with_benkei.jpg; Ieyasu from http://en.wikipedia.org/wiki/Tokugawa_Ieyasu.

33. Chart adapted from Sansom, *A History of Japan to 1334,* page 240; http://fr.wikipedia.org/wiki/Seiwa-Genji; and http://en.wikipedia.org/wiki/Seiwa_Genji.
34. A copy of the manuscript was kindly provided to the author by Dr. Sovik.
35. For more on the Battle of Nagashino, see Christopher M. Clarke, *Warriors and Wisemen.* (Second edition.) Huntingtown, MD: Clarke's Canyon Press, 2011, pages 205-218. See also Yasushi Inoue, *The Samurai Banner of Furin Kazan.* Rutland, VT: Tuttle, (1958) 2005.
36. For more information, see http://www.beisho.org.
37. See "David Diguangco" at http://www.linkedin.com/pub/david-diguangco/3/769/a23; "David Diguangco" at http://www.yatedo.com/p/David+Diguangco/normal/b03474663678c6b504f3c5470d70715e; "United States Classical Kendo Federation" at https://secure.utah.gov/bes/action/details?entity=1281134-0140; David Diguangco, "Kogen Itto Ryu ad thye Concept of Ai-Uchi" from *The Iaido Newsletter*, Volume 6, Number 10, #50 OCT 1994 at http://www.collections-canada.gc.ca/eppp-archive/100/202/300/iaido/1994/tin50.html and numerous postings on various *kendo* Internet forums.
38. "Craig N. Campbell" in *The Columbus Dispatch*, February 11, 2014; postings on the now defunct website of the United States Classical Kendo Federation; and numerous postings on various *kendo* Internet forums.
39. See http://www.thomassovik.com/; "Thomas Sovik" at https://music.unt.edu/faculty-and-staff/detail/107; and several personal email exchanges.
40. My only information about Mr. Wilcoxen is indirectly through Dr. Sovik.
41. Bonnie Engleman, "Martial Arts with Bamboo Swords: Want To? Kendo!" from the *Columbia* [MD] *Flyer*, April 8, 2002; Ernest Lissabet and Donald Seto, Ph.D., "Cherry Blossom Kendo: A Short History of Kendo in Washington D.C." in *Kendo World*, Volume 4.2, June 2008; and "In Memoriam: Dr. William (Bill) Dvorine" at http://lotsofocelots.blogspot.com/2013/07/in-memoriam-dr-william-bill-dvorine.html. Dvorine published at least two articles in *Black Belt Magazine*: "How Safe Is Kendo?", (September 1978) and "Sensible Solutions to Rash Prob-

lems" (December 1979), and a book on dermatology (*A Dermatologist's Guide to Home Skin Treatment*, 1984). He was a member of the Physicians Martial Arts Association and the Judo Black Belt Federation of the United States.

42. Internet forum posting, July 8, 2009. See also "Donald Yehling" at http://www.linkedin.com/pub/donald-yehling/17/806/517; "Yobukan Kenjutsu" at https://sites.google.com/site/yobukan-kenjutsu/; and a number of postings on Internet *kendo* forums.
43. "Donald M. Yehling," *The Columbus Dispatch*, September 27, 2013.
44. Paper in the author's possession.
45. Internet posting from September 2004 by A.J. Bryant, a student of Kotaka from 1995-1999.
46. Phil Fellman, Ph.D. "Dr. Kotaka Sadao, Headmaster, *Sakurai-ha Kohgen Itto-Ryu*."
47. *Ibid.*
48. *Ibid.*
49. Grammar as posted. http://www.kendo-world.com/forum/search?searchJSON=%7B%22keywords%22%3A%22kotaka%22%2C%22sort%22%3A%7B%22relevance%22%3A%22desc%22%7D%2C%22view%22%3A%22%22%2C%22exclude_type%22%3A%5B%22vBForum_PrivateMessage%22%5D%7D&btnSubmit=&humanverify%5Binput%5D=bokken&humanverify%5Bhash%5D=d4b9df840db8348841360238d287c29b&humanverify%5Binput%5D=bokken&humanverify%5Bhash%5D=d4b9df840db8348841360238d287c29b.
50. Phil Fellman, "A Visit with the Classical Kendo Federation," web posting from *The Iaido Newsletter*, Volume 9, Number 3 #79, March, 1997. These comments coincide exactly with my recollection of *keiko* with Kotaka *Sensei*. While always decisive, his scores were never harsh or excessively strong.

Notes to Part II

1. William Scott Wilson, (trans. and ed.). *The Swordsman's Handbook: Samurai Teachings on the Path of the Sword.* Boston: Shambhala, 2014, page 8.
2. See for example, Willem Bekink, *Legacy of the Gods: Classical Traditions of Japanese Swordsmanship*. Delft: Uitgeverji, 2013, pages 12-13. For the original myths, see Basil Hall Chamberlain (trans.), *The Kojiki: Records of Ancient Matters*. Rutland, VT: Tuttle, (reprint) 2005 and W.G. Aston (trans.), *Nihongi: Chronicles of Japan from the Earliest of Times to A.D. 697*. Rutland, VT: Tuttle, (reprint) 2011.
3. See, for example, Clarke, *Samurai, Scoundrels, and Saints:*

Stories from the Martial Arts, pages 85-87.
4. See Christopher M. Clarke, *Warriors and Wisemen*. (Second edition.) Huntingtown, MD: Clarke's Canyon Press, 2011, pages 25-31.
5. For excellent introductions to the evolution of swords and swordsmanship schools, see G. Cameron Hurst, III, *Armed Martial Arts of Japan: Swordsmanship and Archery*. New Haven, CT: Yale University Press, 1998 and Serge Mol, *Classical Swordsmanship of Japan: A Comprehensive Guide to Kenjutsu and Iaijutsu*. NP: Eibusha, 2010. Bekink, *op. cit.* also has a good, but shorter, introduction.
6. Hurst, *op. cit.* page 35.
7. Bekink, *op. cit.*, page 27. Interestingly, the second catalogue was said to have been compiled by Fujita Seiko, the so-called "last of the *ninja*." For more on Fujita, see Christopher M. Clarke, *Okinawan Kobudo: A History of Weaponry Styles and Masters*. Huntingtown, MD: Clarke's Canyon Press, 2013, pages 127-135. For another count of schools in the Edo era, see Mol, *op. cit.*, pages 73 ff. Mol reports that "Conservative estimates put the total number of [sword] schools at around 200 to 300, others mention some 700 schools, and more bold estimates even speak of 2,000 to 3,000 schools." (page 75.)
8. Mol, *op. cit.*, page 77 names the *Nen-ryu, Shinto-ryu*, and *Kage-ryu* as the three ancestral schools. Bekink (page 28) lists the *Shinto* and *Kage* styles, but substitutes the *Chujo-ryu* and the third, as do Toshinobu Sakai and Alexander Bennett. *A Bilingual Guide to the History of Kendo*. Tokyo: Sukijanaru,2010, page 133. Actually, the *Chujo-ryu* can be traced to the *Nen-ryu*. Hurst (pages 45-52) lists the *Shinto* and *Kage* styles and *Itto-ryu*, but this reflects later developments. Other major styles include the *Enmei-ryu* (apparently founded by Miyamoto Musashi's grandfather) and the *Niten Ichi-ryu*, of Musashi.
9. The following information on *Nen-ryu* is taken from Mol, *op. cit.* (pages 119 ff.) and Bekink, *op. cit.* (page 69) unless otherwise noted. These two sources do not agree on all details. Where they conflict, I have chosen Mol's fuller and probably better researched version.
10. On *Maniwa Nen-ryu*, see Mol, *op. cit.*, pages 120-122; Donn Draeger, *Classical Budo. The Martial Arts and Ways of Japan*. New York: Weatherhill, 1973; Diane Skoss, ed., *Koryu Bujutsu: Classical Warrior Traditions of Japan, Volume 1*. Berkeley Heights, NJ: Koryu Books, 1997; and Diane Skoss, ed., *Keiko Shokon. Classical Warrior Traditions of Japan, Volume 3*. Berkeley Heights, NJ: Koryu Books, 2002.
11. The following information on *Chujo-ryu*, is taken from Mol, *op.*

cit. (pages 126 ff.), Bekink, *op. cit.* (page 46-68), and Sakai and Bennett, *A Bilingual Guide to the History of Kendo*, pages 133-135. See also Meik Skoss, "Itto-ryu Kenjutsu: An Overview" in Diane Skoss, ed., *Keiko Shokon. Classical Warrior Traditions of Japan, Volume 3*, especially pages 109-110. See also the *Chujo-ryu* entry at http://ja.wikipedia.org/wiki/%E4%B8%AD%E6% 9D%A1%E6%B5%81 (in Japanese) and William deLange, *Famous Japanese Swordsmen of the Warring States Period.* Warren, CT: Floating World Editions, 2006, *passim.*

12. Mol, *op. cit.*, page 126.
13. *Ibid.*, page 127. On the various descendant schools he mentions, see *ibid.*, pages 127-130.
14. Meik Skoss, "Itto-ryu Kenjutsu: An Overview," in *Fighting Arts.com*'s "Reading Room" at http://www.fightingarts.com/ reading/article.php?id=370.
15. *Ibid.*
16. The following information, unless otherwise specified, is taken from Mol, *op. cit.*, pages 131-134; Bekink, *op. cit.*, pages 51-55; Hurst, *op. cit.*, pages 50-51; Sakai and Bennett, *A Bilingual Guide to the History of* Kendo, pages 133-135; and Makoto Suga-wara, *Lives of Master Swordsmen.* Tokyo: East Publications, 1985, pages 161-182. Although the most detailed, the latter is also the most "fanciful." See also William Scott Wilson's intro-duction (pages 21-25) to the chapter on Ito Ittosai Kagehisa and Kotoda Yahei Toshitada's article "Ittosai Sensei Kempo Sho" (trans. by Wilson) in William Scott Wilson (trans. & ed.), *The Swordsman's Handbook: Samurai Teachings on the Path of the Sword.* Boston: Shambhala, 2014, pages 25-41.
17. Hiroko Yoda, "Spooky Izu: Tales of sorcerers and suicide on Izu Oshima" at http://travel.cnn.com/tokyo/play/spooky-izu-tales-sorcerers-and-suicide-izu-oshima-041080.
18. *Ibid.* As one tourist website puts it, "Let's be honest: Nobody in their right mind picks Izu Oshima as their first holiday destina-tion. Go ahead, tell a Tokyoite you're shipping out there for the weekend. You might as well tell them you're planning to spend a few days in Timbuktu. The name doesn't exactly fill mainlanders with the warm and fuzzies. Until the early 20th century, social undesirables were banished to the island. More recently it's become associated with the more grisly side of Japanese pop culture. In 'Godzilla 1985,' the Japanese government dumped the eponymous monster into the bubbling caldera of the island's Mount Mihara volcano, and the mother of Sadako in the J-horror classic 'The Ring' was born here." Hiroko Yoda and Matt Alt, "Izu Oshima: The volcanic island that time and Tokyo forgot" at http://travel.cnn.com/tokyo/play/izu-oshima-400758. No wonder

Yagoro wanted to escape.

19. This legend is related in, among other places, Bekink, *op. cit,.* page 52.
20. On Toda Seigen and his school, see Mol., *op. cit.*, pages 127-130.
21. Mol, *op. cit.*, page 132.
22. Interview by David Diguangco, "Sadao Kotaka, Kogen Ito Ryu" in *The Iaido Newsletter,* Volume 7, Number 11, #63, November 1995.
23. Kotoda Yahei Toshitada, "Ittosai Sensei Kenpo Sho" in Wilson, (trans. and ed.). *The Swordsman's Handbook: Samurai Teachings on the Path of the Sword,* page 26.
24. Bekink, *op. cit.*, pages, 53-54.
25. Mol, *op. cit.*, pages 132-133.
26. *Ibid.*
27. Following quotes from Kotoda Yahei Toshitada, "Ittosai Sensei Kenpo Sho" in Wilson, (trans. and ed.). *The Swordsman's Handbook: Samurai Teachings on the Path of the Sword, passim.*
28. Bekink, *op. cit.*, page 54.
29. This rather fanciful version of what may actually have been a challenge match is relayed in Sugawara, *Lives of Master Swordsmen,* page 173-174.
30. *Ibid.*, page 168.
31. For the story of the transmission of the style, see Bekink, *op. cit.*, pages 54-55; Mol, *op. cit.*, page 134; Sugawara, *op. cit.*, pages 178-182; Sakai and Bennett, *A Bilingual Guide to the History of Kendo,* page 135; and Wilson, *The Swordsman's Handbook: Samurai Teachings on the Path of the Sword,* pages 23-24.
32. The following information on Tenzen/Ono, unless otherwise identified, is taken from Serge Mol, *Classical Swordsmanship of Japan: A Comprehensive Guide to Kenjutsu and Iaijutsu.* NP: Eibusha, 2010; Toshinobu Sakai and Alexander Bennett. *A Bilingual Guide to the History of Kendo.* Tokyo: Sukijanaru,2010; Makoto Sugawara, *Lives of Master Swordsmen.* Tokyo: East Publications, 1985; G. Cameron Hurst, III, *Armed Martial Arts of Japan: Swordsmanship and Archery.* New Haven, CT: Yale University Press, 1998; and Willem Bekink, *Legacy of the Gods: Classical Traditions of Japanese Swordsmanship.* Delft: Uitgeverji, 2013. For a detailed account of Ono, see William deLange, *Famous Japanese Swordsmen of the Period of Unification.* Warren, CT: Floating World Editions, 2008, pages 1-126.
33. For information on the *"han"* system, see "Han" at http://wiki.samurai-archives.com/index.php?title=Han; "Han System" at http://en.wikipedia. org/wiki/Han_system; and "List of Han" at http://en.wikipedia.org/wiki/List_of_Han. The latter contains maps and links to descriptions of a number of the feudal *han.*

34. Following story from Mol, *op. cit.*, pages 136-137. See also Sugawara, *op. cit.*, pages 184 ff.
35. Sugawara, *op. cit.*, page 186.
36. Mol, *op. cit.*, page 137.
37. *Ibid.* page 138.
38. *Ibid.*
39. For a couple of stories about the Yagyu family and their relationship to the Tokugawa family, see Clarke, *Samurai, Scoundrels, and Saints*, pages 136-137 and 142-144. For a full treatment, see deLange, *Famous Japanese Swordsmen of the Period of Unification*, pages 127-234.
40. Mol, *op. cit.*, page 138.
41. Sugawara, *op. cit.*, page 197.
42. The information in this paragraph is taken from Kotaka Sadao, "Answer to the Kendo Questions," private paper shared with the author by Dr. Tom Sovik.
43. Guy Buyens, "Ono-ha Itto Ryu" at http://www.hontaiyoshinryu. be/articles/OHIR.pdf. The chronology presented in Buyen's article appears to be off.
44. Regional Cultural Assets Portal, "Bushu Chichibu Kougen-Ittouryu" at http://bunkashisan.ne.jp/search/ViewContent_e.php?from=10&ContentID=353.
45. For information on *Kogen Itto-ryu*, see Hurst, *Armed Martial Arts of Japan: Swordsmanship and Archery*, pages 98-100; Meik Skoss, "Itto-ryu Kenjutsu: An Overview" in Dianne Skoss, ed., *Keiko Shokon. Classical Warrior Traditions of Japan, Volume 3*; Meik Skoss, "Kogen Itto-ryu: An Overview" at http://www. koryu.com/library/mskoss14.html; Kotaka, "Answer to the Kendo Questions"; "Kogen Itto Ryu 甲源一刀流: Itto Ryu of Henmi clan of Kai" (video), part of the *Nihon Budokan* Series (no longer available); and "Kogen Itto-ryu" at https:// www.youtube.com/watch?v=-bcle1NmOEU.
46. Skoss, "Kogen Itto-ryu: An Overview."
47. *Ibid.*
48. Original story from Yamamoto Kunio, *Saitama Bugeicho*. Urawa: Sakitama Suppankai, 1981, related by Hurst, *op. cit.*, pages 98-99.

Notes to Part III

1. The most complete and detailed account of the period in English is Romulus Hillsborough, *Samurai Revolution: The Dawn of Modern Japan Seen Through the Eyes of the Shogun's Last Samurai*. Rutland, VT: Tuttle, 2014. For much fuller treatments

of the period in question than given here, the reader should refer to Marius B. Jansen, *The Making of Modern Japan*. Cambridge, MA: Harvard University, 2000 and Donald Keene, *Emperor of Japan: Meiji and His World, 1852-1912*. New York: Columbia University Press, 2002, the two best treatments of the period. See also George Sansom, *The Western World and Japan*. New York: Random House, 1949.

2. For additional information on more specific aspects of the period, including the Shinsengumi, see Romulus Hillsborough, *Ryoma: Life of a Renaissance Samurai*. San Francisco: Ridgeback Press, 1999; Romulus Hillsborough, *Samurai Sketches From the Bloody Final Years of the Shogun*. San Francisco: Ridgeback Press, 2001; Romulus Hillsborough, *Shinsengumi: The Shogun's Last Samurai Corps*. Rutland, VT: Tuttle, 2005; Romulus Hillsborough, *Samurai Tales: Courage, Fidelity, and Revenge in the Final Years of the Shogun*. Rutland, VT: Tuttle, 2010; Marius Jansen, *Sakamoto Ryoma and the Meiji Restoration*. New York: Columbia University Press, 1995; Mark Ravina, *The Last Samurai: The Life and Battles of Saigo Takamori*. New York: John Wiley and Sons, 2004; and Ryotaro Shiba, *The Last Shogun: The Life of Tokugawa Yoshinobu*. New York: Kodansha, 1988.

3. Hillsborough, *Samurai Sketches From the Bloody Final Years of the Shogun*, page 193.

4. Samurai Wiki, "Shinsengumi" at http://wiki.samurai-archives.com/index.php?title=Shinsengumi.

5. See, for example, John Stevens, *The Sword of No-Sword: Life of the Master Warrior Tesshu*. Boston: Shambhala, 1984.

6. Romulus Hillsborough, *Shinsengumi: The Shogun's Last Samurai Corps*. Rutland, VT: Tuttle, 2005, pages 16-17.

7. See, for example, Hillsborough, *Samurai Revolution* and "Matsudaira, Katamori" at http://en.wikipedia.org/wiki/Matsudaira_Katamori.

8. The following information, unless otherwise specified, is taken from the sources in note 2 above and Hillsborough, *Shinsengumi*; Samurai Wiki, "Shinsengumi" at http://wiki.samurai-archives.com/index.php?title=Shinsengumi; and "Shinsengumi" at http://en.wikipedia.org/wiki/Shinsengumi.

9. See Nobuyuki Hirakami, *Tennen Rishin-ryu Kenjutsu*. Tokyo: BAB Books, 2007.

10. On Serizawa's crimes, see for example, Hillsborough, *Shinsengumi*, page 30; Serizawa Kamo at http://www.shinsengumi-no-makoto.net/serizawa_kamo.htm; and "Shinsengumi—Government Thugs or Embers of a Dying Age" at http://www.chinahistory forum.com/topic/8180-shinsengumi-.

11. Hillsborough, *Shinsengumi*, page 58.

12. See, for example, Hillsborough, *Shisengumi*, pages 71-82.
13. Hillsborough, *Samurai Tales*, page 175.
14. For additional, but very limited, information on Hiruma Yohachi, see Anatoliy Anshin, *The Intangible Warrior Culture of Japan: Bodily Practices, Mental Attitudes, and Values of the Two-sworded Men from the Fifteenth to the Twenty-first Centuries.* Ph.D. Dissertation. Canberra: The University of New South Wales (UNSW), the Australian Defence Force Academy (ADFA), 2009 (citing *Nihon no budo: kendo (jo)* [Japanese *Martial Arts: Swordsmanship (Short Staff)*]. Tokyo: Kodansha, 1983; and Internet post by Lito Ramirez, at http://www.e-budo.com/archive/index.php/t-10874.html.
15. Hokushin Shinoh Ryu Iaido, "100 The Famous Swordsmen From Japan" [*sic.*], http://hokushin. com.au/articles/100-swordsmen/. Both Anshin (page 198) and the Hokushin Shinoh Ryu Iaido article mention "Hiruma Toshi-mitsu," while the latter also lists a "Hiruma Ryouhachi Toshihiro." These apparently were relatives of Yohachi.
16. See "Ito Kashitaro" at http://www.Shinsengumi-no-makoto.net//Ito_Kashitaro.htm.
17. See, for example, "Misc. Shinsengumi Members" at http://www.Shinsengumi-no-makoto.net/misc_shinsengumi_members,htm; and The Samurai Archives at http://wiki.samurai-archives.com/.
18. Kotaka Sukesaburo (Minamotono) Sadayasu (Sadao Kotaka, Ph.D.), "A legend of Sakurai-ha Kaigenji (Kogen) Itto-ryu," paper in the possession of the author.

Bibliography

This is a partial bibliography of books examined for this publication. It is by no means comprehensive.

Bekink, Willem. *Legacy of the Gods: Classical Traditions of Japanese Swordsmanship*. Delft: Uitgeverji, 2013.

Bennett, Alexander, ed. *Budo Perspectives*. Aukland, NZ: Kendo World Publications, 2005.

Berry, Mary Elizabeth. *Hideyoshi*. Cambridge, MA: Harvard University, 1982.

Budden, Paul. *Devil's Glove and the One Cut: An Introduction to Ono -ha Itto-ryu Kata*. Lexington, KY: NP, 2014.

Clarke, Christopher M. *Samurai, Scoundrels, and Saints*. (Second edition.) Huntingtown, MD: Clarke's Canyon Press, 2011.

Clarke, Christopher M. *Warriors and Wisemen*. (Second edition.) Huntingtown, MD: Clarke's Canyon Press, 2011.

Clarke, Christopher M. *Monks, Madmen, and Martial Masters*. (Second edition.) Huntingtown, MD: Clarke's Canyon Press, 2013.

Cleary, Thomas. *The Japanese Art of War: Understanding the Culture of Strategy*. Boston: Shambhala, 1991.

Cleary, Thomas. *Training the Samurai Mind: A Bushido Sourcebook*. Boston: Shambhala, 2008.

Cleary, Thomas. *Samurai Wisdom: Lessons from Japan's Warrior Culture*. Rutland, VT: Tuttle, 2009.

Cleary, Thomas. *Secrets of the Japanese Art of Warfare From the School of Certain Victory*. Rutland, VT: Tuttle, 2012.

Conlan, Thomas D. (trans. and introduction.). *In Little Need of Divine Intervention: Takezaki Suenaga's Scrolls of the Mongol Invasions of Japan*. Ithaca, NY: Cornell University Press, 2001.

Cook, Harry. *Samurai: The Story of a Warrior Tradition*. New York: Sterling Publishers, 1993.

deLange, William. *Famous Japanese Swordsmen of the Warring States Period*. Warren, CT: Floating World Editions, 2006.

deLange, William. *Famous Japanese Swordsmen of the Two Courts Period.* Warren, CT: Floating World Editions, 2007.

deLange, William. *Famous Japanese Swordsmen of the Period of Unification.* Warren, CT: Floating World Editions, 2008.

Dobson, Terry. *It's a Lot Like Dancing: An Aikido Journey.* Berkeley, CA: Blue Snake Books, 1994.

Dometrich, William. *Karate: The Endless Quest.* Los Angeles: Empire Books, 2007.

Friday, Karl. *The First Samurai: The Life and Legend of the Warrior Rebel Taira Masakado.* New York: John Wiley and Sons, 2008.

Friday, Karl. *Hired Swords: The Rise of Private Warrior Power in Early Japan.* Stanford, CA: Stanford University, 1992.

Hillsborough, Romulus. *Ryoma: Life of a Renaissance Samurai.* San Francisco: Ridgeback Press, 1999.

Hillsborough, Romulus. *Samurai Sketches From the Bloody Final Years of the Shogun.* San Francisco: Ridgeback Press, 2001.

Hillsborough, Romulus. *Shinsengumi: The Shogun's Last Samurai Corps.* Rutland, VT: Tuttle, 2005.

Hillsborough, Romulus. *Samurai Tales: Courage, Fidelity, and Revenge in the Final Years of the Shogun.* Rutland, VT: Tuttle, 2010.

Hillsborough, Romulus. *Samurai Revolution: The Dawn of Modern Japan Seen Through the Eyes of the Shogun's Last Samurai.* Rutland, VT: Tuttle, 2014.

Hirakami, Nobuyuki. *Tennen Rishin-ryu Kenjutsu.* Tokyo: BAB Books, 2007.

Hurst, G. Cameron III. *Armed Martial Arts of Japan: Swordsmanship and Archery.* New Haven, CT: Yale University Press, 1998.

Ikegami, Eiko. *The Taming of the Samurai: Honorific Individualism in the Making of Modern Japan.* Cambridge, MA: Harvard University, 1995.

Jansen, Marius. *Sakamoto Ryoma and the Meiji Restoration.* New York: Columbia University Press, 1995.

Jansen, Marius B. *The Making of Modern Japan*. Cambridge, MA: Harvard University, 2000.

Kammer, Reinhard (ed. and annotated.). *The Way of the Sword: The Tengu-Geijutsu-Ron of Chozan Shissai*. Boston, Arkana Press, 1986.

Katsu Kokichi (trans. Teruo Craig.). *Musui's Story: The Autobiography of a Tokugawa Samurai*. Tucson: University of Arizona Press, 1988.

Keene, Donald. *Seeds in the Heart: Japanese Literature from Earliest Times to the Late Sixteenth Century*. New York: Henry Holt, & Co., 1993.

Keene, Donald. *Emperor of Japan: Meiji and His World, 1852-1912*. New York: Columbia University Press, 2002.

Kiyota, Minoru. *The Shambhala Guide to Kendo*. Boston: Shambhala, 2002.

Kure, Mitsuo. *Samurai: An Illustrated History*. Rutland, VT: Tuttle, 2002.

Kure, Mitsuo. *Samurai Arms, Armor, Costume*. Edison, NJ: Chartwell Books, 2007.

Kyou Ichisuke, *Iai no Ryuha: Techniques & Features of Well-Known Schools*. (In Japanese.) Tokyo: Airyudo, 2010.

Lovret, Frederick J. *The Way and the Power: Secrets of Japanese Strategy*. Boulder, CO: Paladin Press, 1987.

Lowry, Dave. *Traditions: Essays on the Japanese Martial Arts and Ways*. Rutland, VT: Tuttle, 2002.

Lowry, Dave. *Autumn Lightning: The Education of An American Samurai*. Boston: Shambhala, 1985.

Man, John. *Samurai: The Last Warrior*. New York: William Morrow, 2014.

McCullough, Helen Craig (trans. and introduction.). *The Taiheiki: A Chronicle of Medieval Japan*. Rutland, VT: Tuttle, 1959.

McCullough, Helen Craig (trans. and introduction.). *Yoshitsune: A*

Fifteenth-Century Japanese Chronicle. Stanford, CA: Stanford University, 1971.

McCullough, Helen Craig. *The Tale of the Heike.* Stanford: Stanford University Press, 1988.

McCullough, Helen Craig. *Genji and Heike. Selections from "The Tale of Genji" and "The Tale of the Heike".* Stanford: Stanford University Press, 1994.

Miller, David. *Samurai Warriors.* New York: St. Martins Press, 1999.

Mol, Serge. *Classical Swordsmanship of Japan: A Comprehensive Guide to Kenjutsu and Iaijutsu.* NP: Eibusha, 2010.

Morris, Ivan. *The Nobility of Failure: Tragic Heroes in the History of Japan.* New York: Farrar, Straus & Giroux, 1975.

Nakamura, Taisaburo. *The Spirit of the Sword: Iaido, Kendo, and Test Cutting with the Japanese Sword.* Berkeley, CA: Blue Snake Books, 1980/2013.

Nakazato, Kaizan. *Bodhisattva Toge (Boddhisatva Pass).* (In Japanese.) Tokyo: Shinjusha, 1929.

Nihon no-Kenjutsu. (Japanese Swordsmanship, in Japanese), Tokyo: Gakken, 2007.

Nitobe, Inazo. *Bushido: The Soul of Japan.* Los Angeles: Ohara Publications, 1969.

Perrin, Noel. *Giving Up the Gun: Japan's Reversion to the Sword, 1543-1879.* Boston: David R. Godine, 1979.

Rabinovitch, Judith (trans. and ed.). *Shomonki: The Story of Masakado's Rebellion.* Tokyo: Sophia University, 1986.

Ravina, Mark. *The Last Samurai: The Life and Battles of Saigo Takamori.* New York: John Wiley and Sons, 2004.

Richie, Donald. *Memoirs of the Warrior Kumagai: A Historical Novel.* Rutland, VT: Tuttle, 1998.

Sadler, A.L. *The Maker of Modern Japan: The Life of Tokugawa Ieyasu.* New York: Taylor & Francis, 1937/2010.

Sadler, A.L. *The Code of the Samurai.* Rutland, VT: Tuttle, 1941/1988.

Sadler, A.L. (trans.) *The Ten Foot Square Hut and Tales of the Heike.* Rutland, VT: Tuttle, 1972.

Sakai, Toshinobu and Alexander Bennet. *A Bilingual Guide to the History of Kendo.* Tokyo: Sukijanaru, 2010.

Sansom, George. *The Western World and Japan.* New York: Random House, 1949.

Sansom, George. *A History of Japan to 1334.* Stanford, CA: Stanford University, 1958.

Sansom, George. *A History of Japan 1334-1615.* Stanford, CA: Stanford University, 1961.

Sasamori Junzo and Gordon Warner. *This Is Kendo: The Art of Japanese Fencing.* Rutland, VT: Tuttle, 1964.

Sato, Hiroaki. *Legends of the Samurai.* Woodstock, NY: The Overlook Press, 1995.

Sato, Hiroaki (trans. and introduction). *The Sword and the Mind: The Classic Japanese Treatise of Swordsmanship and Tactics.* New York: Barnes and Noble, 1985.

Skoss, Diane, ed. *Keiko Shokon: Classical Warrior Traditions, Volume 3.* Berkeley Heights, NJ: Koryu Books, 1999.

Sharpe, Michael. *Samurai Leaders From the Tenth to the Nineteenth Century.* New York: Metro Books, 2008.

Shiba, Ryotaro. *The Last Shogun: The Life of Tokugawa Yoshinobu.* New York: Kodansha, 1988.

Storry, Richard. *The Way of the Samurai.* New York: Putman, 1978.

Sugawara, Makoto. *Lives of Master Swordsmen.* Tokyo: East Publications, 1985.

Sugawara, Sadamoto. (Trans. Eric Shahan). *The Complete Martial Arts of Japan: Volume One, Gekken.* NP: NP, 2014.

Sugimoto, Etsu Inagaki. *A Daughter of the Samurai: How a Daughter of Feudal Japan, Living Hundreds of Years in One Generation, Became a Modern American.* Rutland, VT: Tuttle, 1966.

Tabata, Kazumi. *Secret Tactics: Lessons from the Great Masters of Martial Arts.* Rutland, VT: Tuttle, 2003.

Totman, Conrad. *Tokugawa Ieyasu, Shogun: A Biography.* Torrence, CA: Heian International, 1983.

Turnbull, Stephen. *The Samurai: A Military History.* New York: Macmillan, 1977.

Turnbull, Stephen. *The Book of the Samurai: The Warrior Class of Japan.* New York: Gallery Books, 1982.

Turnbull, Stephen. *Samurai Warriors.* London: Blandford Press, 1987.

Turnbull, Stephen. *Battles of the Samurai.* London: Arms and Armour Press, 1987.

Turnbull, Stephen. *Samurai Warlords: The Book of the Daimyo.* London: Blandford Press, 1989.

Turnbull, Stephen. *The Samurai and the Sacred.* London: Arms and Armour Press, 1990.

Turnbull, Stephen. *Samurai Warfare.* London: Arms and Armour Press, 1996.

Turnbull, Stephen. *The Samurai Sourcebook.* London: Arms and Armour Press, 1998.

Turnbull, Stephen. *Samurai: The World of the Warrior.* New York: Osprey, 2003.

Turnbull, Stephen. *Samurai: The Story of Japan's Great Warriors.* New York: Sterling Press, 2004.

Turnbull, Stephen. *Warriors of Medieval Japan.* New York: Osprey, 2005.

Turnbull, Stephen. *The Lone Samurai and the Martial Arts.* New York: Osprey, 2006.

Turnbull, Stephen. *The Samurai Swordsman: Master of War*. Rutland, VT: Tuttle, 2008.

Turnbull, Stephen. *Tokugawa Ieyasu*. New York: Osprey, 2012.

Uki, Terukuni. *Junichi Haga's Secrets of Kendo*, Vol 1., *Kendo Jidai*, July-Sep. 2006 (electronic version).

Uki, Terukuni. *Junichi Haga's Secrets of Kendo*, Vol 2., *Kendo Jidai*, (electronic version), 2012.

Varley, Paul. *Warriors of Japan As Portrayed in the War Tales*. Honolulu: University of Hawaii, 1994.

Warner, Gordon and Donn F. Draeger. *Japanese Swordsmanship: Technique and Practice*. New York: Weatherhill, 1983.

Wilson, William Scott (trans. and introduction). *Ideals of the Samurai: Writings of Japanese Warriors*. Santa Clarita, CA: Ohara Publications, 1982.

Wilson, William Scott (trans.). *The Life-Giving Sword: Secret Teachings from the House of the Shogun*. New York: Kodansha, 2003.

Wilson, William Scott (trans.). *The Demon's Sermon on the Martial Arts* (of Issai Chozanshi). New York: Kodansha, 2006.

Wilson, William Scott (trans.). *Yojokun: Life Lessons from a Samurai* (Kaibara Ekiken). New York: Kodansha, 2009.

Wilson, William Scott (trans. and ed.). *The Swordsman's Handbook: Samurai Teachings on the Path of the Sword*. Boston: Shambhala, 2014.

Wilson, William R. (trans. and annotated). *Hogen Monogatari: Tale of the Disorder in Hogen*. Tokyo: Sophia University, 1971.

Yamamoto, Tsunetomo (trans. William Scott Wilson.). *Hagakure: The Book of the Samurai*. New York: Kodansha, 1983.

Yoshikawa, Eiji. *The Heike Story*. Rutland, VT: Tuttle, 1956.

Yoshikawa, Eiji. *Musashi: An Epic Novel of the Samurai Era*. New York: Kodansha, (reprint) 2012.

Yoshikawa, Eiji. *Taiko: An Epic Novel of War and Glory in Feudal Japan.* New York: Kodansha, (reprint) 2012.

Films (all based on *Kogen Itto-ryu Kenjutsu*)

Dai Bosatsu Toge, Dai Ippen, Kogen Itto-ryu no Maki (1935). Director: Inagaki Hiroshi.

Dai Bosatsu Toge, Suzuko-yama no Maki, Mibu Shiabara no Maki (1936). Director: Inagaki Hiroshi.

Dai Bosatsu Toge Dai Ichibu (*The Great Buddha Pass: Part I, Souls in the Moonlight*), 1957. Director: Uchida Tomu.

Satan's Sword: Dai Bosatsu Toge (*The Great Buddha Pass*), Part 1 (1960). Director: Misumi Kenji.

Satan's Sword: Ryujin no Maki (*The Dragon God*), Part 2 (1960). Director: Misumi Kenji.

Satan's Sword: Kanketsu Hen (*The Final Chapter*), Part 3 (1960). Director: Mori Kazuo.
Dai Bosatsu Toge (*Sword of Doom*), (1966). Director: Okamoto Kihachi.

Shinsengumi: Assassins of Honor, (1970). Director: Sawashima Tadashi.

When the Last Sword Is Drawn, (2003). Director: Takita Yojiro.

Kogen Itto Ryu Kenjutsu. Nihon Kobudo Series, (2005).

Kotaka Sukesaburo Minamoto-no Sadayasu Sadao
(1933-2013)

武士は死せず、唯刀の匂となるのみ

"A *samurai* never dies. He just becomes the hue of the sword."
Sakurai Gennoshin Fumitaka

Made in the USA
Lexington, KY
29 November 2014